John Nosler—Going Ballistic

John Nosler—Going Ballistic

By John Nosler as told to Gary Lewis

John Nosler—Going Ballistic
By John Nosler as told to Gary Lewis
Copyright © 2005, 2008 by Gary Lewis

ISBN-10: 0-9761244-0-8
ISBN-13: 978-0-9761244-0-5
Second Edition

Cover design by Chevalier Advertising, Lake Oswego, Oregon
Interior by Tightline Design, tightlinedesign.com

Gary Lewis Outdoors
PO Box 1364, Bend, Oregon 97709
541–317–0116

NOSLER, PARTITION, BALLISTIC TIP and SOLID BASE are registered trademarks of Nosler, Inc. The phrases TROPHY GRADE BULLETS, PRACTICAL PISTOL, BULLETS FOR SPORTSMEN, SPORTING HANDGUN, TEST THE BEST, BULLETS FOR THE BIG BOYS, VARMINT PAK, CUSTOM COMPETITION and S.H.O.T.S are trademarks of Nosler, Inc.

CT, BALLISTIC SILVERTIP, PARTITION GOLD, and PARTITION–HG are joint registered trademarks of Nosler, Inc. and Olin–Winchester.

WINCHESTER, SUPREME, SILVERTIP, FAIL SAFE and LUBALOX are registered trademarks of Olin–Winchester.

Dedication

This book is dedicated to my family, my employees, and my friends.
You have supported me throughout this wonderful adventure, and I will
always be indebted to you. I also dedicate this book to hunters, shooters,
and handloaders everywhere. I am grateful for your willingness to try new
ideas, for you have given me a long and satisfying career

~ John Nosler

CONTENTS

Foreword by Chub Eastman ix

Introduction by Gary Lewis... xiii

From Ruffles to Short Pants... 1

Grease Under My Fingernails 7

Gunpowder and Crankshafts.. 15

Working Hard, Playing Hard 17

Work, Wedding Rings, and Responsibility.................................... 25

North to Oregon—A Ford Coupe and Too Much Credit 29

Elk, Ammunition, and Amigos... 41

Moose, a Mountie, and John Henderson 47

Gas Rationing, Lever Guns, and Leverage 53

Penetration and Expansion—The Need for a Better Bullet 59

Partitions on a Pie Plate... 65

One Shot, One Moose... 69

It Worked, So Now What?.. 83

Bull's-eyes, Blacktails and aPartner in the Bullet Business............ 99

Bumpy Going in Canada and Crowfoot....................................... 105

The Industrial Committee 111

A Bullet and a Grizz 117

Accuracy is a Frame of Mind 125

Getting It Right—Perfecting thePartition and Zipedo.................. 135

To the Yukon for Moose, Caribou, and Grizzly 141

42 Grains of Hot Steel.. 151

Copper, Computers, and Chronographs in the Corporate World ... 157

The Ballistic Tip 167

Contents (cont.)

Into Handgunning and Muzzleloading 173

Back to BC—Roughing it in the Rockies 177

Return to Family Ownership 187

A Suit, a Clean White Shirt and a New Bride 191

Bullets, Ballistics, and Big Game 193

Making the AccuBond 209

On Business 213

Constitution and Community—Looking to the Future 219

Back to the Territories—60 Years Later By Gary Lewis 225

Acknowledgements 243

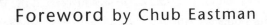

Foreword by Chub Eastman

I settled down, back against a log, elbows on knees to steady the binoculars and focused on the drama that was taking place across the narrow valley in front of me.

By chance, my guide and I had just topped the ridge and climbed off our horses below the skyline to glass the valley for elk. Two large bulls were slowly working their way up a cut line on the far hillside. From our vantage point, the range was close to 800 yards so we just sat, watched and started to discuss a strategy when we spotted John and Bob Nosler, with their guides, at the base of the hill below the elk.

We turned from hunters to privileged observers as the saga unfolded in front of us.

Their range to the bulls was approximately 150 yards and increasing with each step the bulls took. Bob knelt and prepared to shoot. John, with his rifle slung over his shoulder, watched until Bob's bull went down. It wasn't till that point John unslung his .338 Win. Mag. and prepared to make his shot. By this time the second bull was at least 250 yards up the hill.

As we watched, the bull crumpled and started to slide down hill before the sound of the shot reached us.

Back in camp that night, the conversation centered around the day's activities and the success John and Bob had in collecting their elk. Not one time did I hear John say anything about what a hell of a shot he had made, or the patience he exhibited making sure Bob's elk was down before he took the rifle off his shoulder. His comments were directed as to what fine trophies they had collected and what a great job their guides did in finding the elk and packing them back to camp. He enjoyed the adventure of seeing other animals, Mother Nature's grandeur and the camaraderie of his hunting companions. It was obvious to me he enjoyed the hunt for what it was; collecting a fine bull elk was secondary.

This was a side of John that not many people are privileged to see. The other side of John is what anyone in the shooting sports industry relates to.

Thanks to a mud–caked moose in northern British Columbia he saw a need for a bullet that could withstand magnum velocities and penetrate to the vitals. With no fancy formal education and just an innovative idea he created the Partition bullet in 1948 that all premium bullets manufactured today use as a benchmark.

You would think that would be enough to satisfy most anyone. However, when you have an active and inventive mind to go with a love of our sport, new ideas and products just keep coming.

At the age of 91, John still has that inquisitive twinkle in his eye and visits his office every day. Sometimes to read his mail and sometimes to bounce an idea off anyone who will listen. John hasn't changed much over the years. He can still solve

Chub Eastman with an interior grizzly he killed at 15 paces. Surprised at close range on his moose kill, the bear stood on his hind legs to face Chub, ready to fight. A Nosler Partition bullet helped end the standoff. Afterward, Chub found the carcass of another grizzly that the great bear had killed.

a bullet design problem on a napkin at lunch and still shoot the eye out of a prairie dog at 200 yards.

For most of us who have made the shooting sports a career we know the icons in our industry. There is no doubt that John Nosler is one of those gifted few whose contribution to shooters and hunters around the world will always be recognized.

I feel honored to have shared many a campfire and worked with John for over 20 years. As you read his life story you will come to understand why anyone who has spent time with John loves him for who he is even more than what he has accomplished.

Introduction by Gary Lewis

I met John Nosler in 1997 when I showed up for work at Nosler Incorporated on my first day as the corporate buyer. He was the tall, white–haired angular genius that conceived and built the revolutionary Partition bullet and whose work made my job possible. It has been my great good fortune to get to know him better.

In 1946, his foresight, innate engineering know–how, and hard work gave birth to the premium bullet industry, which would come to employ thousands of people across the country and satisfy shooters around the world.

In 2003, I met with Chub Eastman and Matt Smith, both of them admirers of the man they call Big John. Chub, upon retiring from Nosler, Inc, has become an outdoor writer and has since been widely published in the shooting sports magazines. Matt Smith, after working in various departments within the company, left to create his own place in the world of real estate and construction. Both men are accomplished big game hunters, the kind of men that other hunters look up to. Chub and Matt thought that someone should write Big John's story and they elected me.

No project like this is completed without the assistance of many others. My wife, Merrilee, worked long hours, transcribing conversations. Bob Nosler put a lot of time and effort into making sure I had everything I needed. Ron Nosler checked my spelling and made sure I had my facts right. Thanks Bob and Ron, I appreciate your friendship. Bill Lewis, Ed Neff and Alan Ashforth gave of their time. Ed Park, whose pictures of John ended up in a few places in this book, was a big help. Ludo Wurfbain, of Safari Press, reviewed the project and provided encouragement and insight. Thank you to Don Gulbrandson and Ken Ramage, at Krause Publications for your enthusiasm for the project. Thank you to Jay Langston and Harris Andrews at Stoeger Publishing for your advice and support. Thank you to Paul Parsons and Lindsey Brock for reading the book and helping to make it that much better.

Cameron Prow edited the manuscript and helped me see things a different way. Thank you to James Flaherty and Brian Flaherty with Tightline Design for your work in layout. Thank you to Chevalier Advertising for your work on the cover. Thank you to Jason Milliken of Global Publishing Services for guidance along the way.

Most of all, I want to say thank you to John and Vivian Nosler who were the most gracious of hosts on many afternoons spent in their beautiful home. I enjoyed all our conversations and sat spellbound as John recounted stories from many years ago, tales of moose, elk, grizzly bear, guns, bullets, beat up trucks and old friends.

In this book, those stories are told again, in John's words, so you can hear them as I heard them.

Gary Lewis is an outdoor writer and publisher who makes his home in Bend, Oregon. His award-winning articles are published in newspapers and magazines across the country.

He is the author of *Black Bear Hunting, Deer Hunting Tactics for Today's Big Game Hunter, Hunting Oregon, Freshwater Fishing Oregon & Washington*. For more information, visit www.GaryLewisOutdoors.com

CHAPTER I

From Ruffles to Short Pants

September 1946

When I saw him I was too damn close. Behind a screen of willows, the big moose stood broadside. His polished antlers gleamed and his body was black with caked mud. I heard the rasp of his breath and smelled the marsh and the sweat caked on his body. I'd be gored on his antlers if he decided to charge. I snicked the safety to "fire" on my Winchester Model 70 300 H&H Magnum and snugged the butt against my shoulder.

I settled the crosshair in the pocket behind his front leg and took the slack out of the trigger. I squeezed, rocking with the recoil and cycled the bolt. The bull stepped forward and turned his head in my direction and I shot him again. He didn't stagger or fall or bellow and charge. Instead, he turned away and started, at a trot, into the trees. I hit him again, then again and saw him stumble at the impact of the fourth bullet.

I reloaded as I followed in his tracks. I knew my bullets had struck, but it would take several more shots to do the job. The bull was quartering away when I fired again. I stood and fired, working the bolt and fired once more. When the bull was finally on the ground, I stepped close, approaching from behind, ready to fire again if need be.

My friend and guide, Johnny Henderson, helped me with the skinning and we counted the holes, finding that my bullets had struck, but splattered, on the hard, mud–caked shoulder. My 300 H&H had sent its bullets at such high speed that the thin copper jacket couldn't contain the soft lead core. Though I was shooting from close range, most of my shots didn't even penetrate to the vitals. My new, high–powered rifle was too powerful to kill a moose with the bullets available to hunters in the 1940s. Either I had to go back to hunting with my old 30–40 Krag and 30–30 Winchester, or build a better bullet.

On April 4, 1913, Byrd and Perna Nosler welcomed me, their fifth child, into the world. I was born John Amos Nosler in Brawley, California, in a house that smelled of honeydew melon, homemade bread, and butter in the churn.

My father was born on the Oregon Trail, and grew up in Coquille (pronounced Co–keel), Oregon, where his father homesteaded. As a young man, Pop moved south to California's Imperial Valley to try his hand at raising cantaloupes, honeydew melons, and little barefoot farmers.

Our ranch was less than 30 miles from the border with Mexico and not far from the Colorado River which marks the Arizona line. When I was quite young, our land was flooded by the Colorado River, which washed away all our topsoil, and any chance at raising a crop. So Pop bought a cattle ranch in Durango, Colorado, and we pulled up stakes and moved.

The youngest of five children, I had a lot of people looking out for me. Wann was the oldest of us kids, fifteen years my elder. He loved the ranch life, riding horses and working cattle. My sister Hazel was next in line. Sister Ardyce passed away while still a child and Eula was my parents' fourth.

In those days, little boys were made to wear dresses and since we had so many girls in our family, I had plenty of lace and ruffles for my first few years. When I got a little older Mom dressed me in short pants. When she gave me my first pair of long pants, I finally felt I was making some progress. As we got older, we wore bib overalls much of the time. There weren't a lot of shoes to go around so we ran barefoot most of the year.

When I was three years old, we moved from Durango to a big alfalfa ranch in Bishop, California. Bishop sits between the Sierras on the west and the White Mountains to the east. We moved our furniture and tools there in a string of wagons and an old Maxwell car. Being small, I got to ride in the car quite a bit on the way out to California with the mule–drawn wagons following. Sometimes Wann and Pop and a few others would get out front and clear the road so the car could get through the ruts and around trees.

In Bishop we raised horses, mules and alfalfa. Anytime I smell fresh–mown hay I remember those days. Dad knew a war was brewing and raised as many mules as he could, figuring the government would need the animals. The city of Los Angeles

Byrd Nosler, milking cows with Eula (left) and John (right). Eula said, "Come on Papa, you have enough milk in your bucket." 1914

Perna Nosler with daughter Eula and baby John. The noon whistle blew just as the shutter was snapped, capturing the startled look on John's face. 1913

Eula and John

bought water rights from every rancher in the watershed and piped the water down to the city. Things dried up in a big hurry. Pop said he got more money for the water rights on the ranch than the ranch was worth. Mules became our main crop from then until the war hit. Dad was right about the war, eventually selling close to a hundred animals to the government when the United States entered World War I.

Wann took a bunch of stock into Nevada and sold them. He stayed for awhile and drove four– and eight–horse teams pulling fresnos (machines for leveling farmland). We leveled our own alfalfa fields with a fresno and moved a lot of dirt that way, scooping and leveling. The driver would just holler out "Gee" or "Haw," and the horses would turn right or left.

We also used horses to pull wagons loaded with grain out of the hayfields, often a team of ten, sometimes as many as fifteen. You wouldn't have any lines on them at all, except for one rope called a "jerk line." You'd jerk once and the horses would go one way. Jerk twice and they'd go the other. The horse in the lead guided all rest.

I wasn't old enough to do that kind of work for awhile, but I did manage to build a small wagon which I harnessed to a little goat that I had. I drove him around the yard just like my big brother was doing with horses out in the fields.

Dad figured out how to make money ranching and selling real estate so he moved us around quite a bit. From Bishop, we moved to Pomona, with the San Gabriel Mountains to the north and the city of Los Angeles growing out to meet us. When Dad wanted to live a little closer to the water he had sold, he bought a hardware store in town.

From there we moved to central California between Orland and Artois where we had a small dairy about a mile off the highway. Pop and Wann delivered fresh milk from house to house.

Dad was great with a shotgun. I marveled at how he could take a bird in the air. He hunted pheasants and quail when we had them close to the ranch. To supplement his income, he shot ducks for the market and sent them to San Francisco, bringing home extra pennies for the family.

We had an Overland car and a Model T pickup. Automobiles were still new and exciting, and unreliable in those days. There was always an opportunity to learn how they worked while fixing them up. From an early age I had my head under the hood of whatever car my dad owned. When we needed to replace a broken part, we often just fabricated it from something else that was broken down on the place.

During the winter, it was Wann's job to get our Model T jacked up, pour hot water in the radiator and crank it with the wheels off the ground so he could drive us to school.

Sometimes Eula and I would walk to the one–room schoolhouse. I sat on the left side of the class with four or five other first grade kids. Our school was in an old wooden building with a large stove into which the teacher would throw great big chunks of oak and cottonwood. One night the building caught fire and burnt the schoolhouse clear to the ground. So Mom and my older sisters had to teach Eula and me at home for a whole year until a new concrete schoolhouse could be built. Neither the teacher nor us students could burn that one down, no matter how hard we tried.

CHAPTER 2

Grease Under My Fingernails

The year I was seven, Pop bought a ranch three miles out of Huntington Beach on the main road toward Santa Ana. It had a nice house, with a barn and corral. We didn't cultivate the alfalfa there. Dad built a service station instead. The station had a telephone and since most of the ranches in the area didn't have one, people came from all over to use it.

When I was eight my dad took in an old car called a Dort that needed some service work. The owner never paid for the repairs, so Pop kept the car. He said, "John, you can play with it," but I don't think he ever guessed I could get it going again. It was sitting around without a battery. I managed to find an old battery in a wrecked car and was able to get the Dort started. Pop let me drive it around the backyard because I wasn't old enough to drive on the street.

After I sold the Dort, I decided to get a Model T Ford. It was common to see neglected Model Ts in the backyards of ranches, so I rode around on my bicycle until I found one in the backyard of an old clapboard farmhouse. I went up to the door and asked the lady if she wanted to sell it. She said, "I don't know. I guess we don't have any use for it anymore." I asked her if she could use a bicycle. She said that one of her kids needed one, so I traded my bike for the Model T and had a heck of a time bringing it home with some of Dad's mules. After a few days, I managed to get it going and later fixed it up enough to sell.

My dad was not mechanically inclined nor did he ever want to be, but he was good at business. In 1923 he bought a brand–new Cadillac. Behind the service station we had a grease rack we used to service the cars. With the car on this rack, we had room to crawl beneath it and drain the oil. Dad's Cadillac had alumite grease fittings and he knew I liked mechanic work so he had me help him. There were hundreds of these fittings on his car. Pop said, "John, you grease this thing up good so we never have to do it again." I was fortunate to discover my life's work at an early age, mixing mechanics, engineering, and hunting. Even as a little boy I loved mechanical parts and the way everything worked together.

Pop gave me a Daisy pump BB gun and taught me how to shoot it. Along the road, we had a long line of trees that were full of blackbirds. I'd bring a few birds home and my mom would cook some for me. Blackbird was pretty good eating. My dad was so proud of my marksmanship that he bought me a single–shot Benjamin Pump air rifle. No blackbird was safe after that.

Pop's service station was profitable and he made money in real estate for a few years. There was a lot of activity in real estate because there were oil deposits all around. Pop tried desperately to get an oil well on our place but he could never quite make it, so he and the neighbors joined together and purchased some land adjoining ours and put up a derrick. Then they dug a big reservoir and installed the rest of the equipment every oil well had that put a lot of water in to flush the oil out. Some

The family Cadillac, loaded up for a camping trip to California's Big Bear in 1924.

men from the oil companies came to look at it, but for some reason no one wanted to drill a hole. It wasn't because there wasn't oil down there, because I visited later on vacation and the whole place was full of oil wells.

Living on a ranch we always had enough to eat, though money was sometimes scarce. These days most people don't know what it's like to have a pail of fresh warm milk, skim off the cream, and make your own butter and ice cream. We gathered fresh eggs from the chickens and killed or traded for a pig when we needed pork. We were well off whether we had money or not.

For breakfast we almost always had hot mush. I never cared for ham and eggs but Pop loved them. He always had ham and eggs and Mom made me mush and hotcakes. We had a bunch of cows that provided our milk, from which Mom made all our butter. Mom raised one cow from a calf, and we had that one for a long time. That darn cow moved with us, even when we went to the Los Angeles area, when my dad bought a development there.

Mom would pour the fresh milk into a special bowl that let the cream rise to the top. We churned the cream to make butter and made ice cream with it in the summer. I was good at churning butter and made the mistake of bragging about it one day. I ended up doing a lot of churning after that.

My mom made her apple pies in an old wood stove with a big oven that had a water tank on the right–hand side. There were water pipes that circulated water in the hot tank, keeping the water always boiling when the stove was full of wood.

It was hard work to keep your groceries cold in California in those days. We kept our perishable food and homemade ice cream in an icebox. You could only get ice when you went to town. It was the last thing we picked up on our way back to the ranch. We strapped it on the running board of the car and ran for home before much of it could melt. Then Pop would put it in the icebox.

Mom made the soap we washed with and used for laundry. Dad built her an open–air fireplace with a big washtub on top. We'd put water in the tub and she would build a little fire beneath it. She'd peel some soap off and put it in the boiling water, then add the clothes and stir them back and forth. Someone came around selling a washing machine that was about three feet wide, square, with a round tank inside and a big paddle. Dad bought it and Mom showed me how to use it. I got pretty good at doing laundry. That was a real boon for my mom.

I got the croup as a kid. Mom would make a poultice of hot peppers inside a bag of cheesecloth and paste that on my chest. She'd also give me a tiny bit of coal oil with medicine in it. The coal oil was supposed to clean your throat out. I can't imagine what it really did to me. All the kids on the nearby farms wore asafetida bags around their necks to ward off infection and colic. The asafetida was made from a bitter, odorous resin that was as better at warding off other people than it was at keeping us healthy. Home remedies—everybody had them when I was a kid, because no one had ever heard of health insurance.

We went to church on a regular basis. Afterwards, relatives came over to our house or we would all go to theirs.

John and Eula in Huntington Beach.

When I was ten years old, Pop bought a small dairy in Pomona with about 40 head of cows. We'd get up, all of us, about 4 a.m. and start milking. We'd finish milking by 7:00 and move on to the rest of our chores. I had to clean all the milk out and sterilize the tools in a hot tank. We had a big old iron drum that we boiled all the milk buckets in. After I was done cleaning the equipment, I separated the cream from the milk with a machine called a "separator."

A dairy seems to attract cats from all over the county and we always had a lot of them around. Those darn cats would lie around there, just waiting for someone to spill a little milk. We strained the milk through cotton. We kept big rolls of cotton in a tidy cabinet. You'd pull it off a roll like paper and cut it with some scissors. I'd just throw that outside and first thing you'd know the cats would be dragging it around and in two or three days they'd be dragging it out their other ends.

John with the wagon he built on the ranch in Pomona.

We lived in Pomona for a long time. We had relatives there and my Uncle Will Van Horn had a huge dairy outside Ontario with 250 milking cows. I always had a summer job working for my uncle—milking cows, mowing and raking hay, and everything else he could find for me to do. I mowed and raked an awful lot of hay. I'd leave it in the row for someone else with a wagon to pick up. They'd drive to the barn and run the hay through a chopper, then blow it up into the hayloft.

My uncle also raised corn. It was chopped up and blown into his big silos, which could hold 100 tons. The corn was sold for livestock feed. It fermented and once it did that you could keep it forever. The cows loved it. So did the ducks and chickens. Moisture seeped out the sides of the silos and we had fun watching chickens and ducks drink that stuff and get drunk, wobble around the yard, and fall down.

Hoof–and–mouth disease was a very serious problem for ranchers. Coming home from school every day, we had to walk through a pool of inch–deep disinfectant. When an auto or a wagon came up the drive, they had to drive slowly through the disinfectant to kill the germs on the tire rubber.

For entertainment, we went to the movie house on a Saturday, or to the horse races in Pomona. During the L.A. County Fair, we would go every day. In the evenings, we'd listen to the radio then go to bed early to be ready for work the next day.

Wherever we lived, we had a little blacksmith shop on the ranch. I did an awful lot of mowing machine repairs and sharpened sickles on a big white grindstone. Those sickles were seven feet long; each blade had to be sharpened on both sides. I got pretty good at that.

On the ranch, something was always busted and you had to fix it with what you had. This experience was good for me because it taught me to understand machinery and figure out how it worked.

I bought my first single–shot Stevens Favorite 22 when I was still in fifth grade. I think I paid less than $5 for it. I still remember going down to the mailbox, about a quarter of a mile from the house, and finding my new gun from Montgomery Ward waiting for me.

My dad liked to shoot a double–barrel shotgun and he taught me how to use it when I was old enough to handle the recoil. Someone gave me a revolver, too. I never had a lot of cartridges for it, but liked to shoot it when I had the chance.

There were always a few dogs on the ranch, but my best hunting partner was a mutt with a curled–up tail and ears like a police dog. I called him Slick. We hunted rabbits, but what Slick was really good at was catching skunks.

We had a huge alfalfa field irrigated by standpipes along the outer edge. Galvanized pipes carried water from the edge of the field to the middle. Extra pipes were always lying around. Skunks would crawl in those pipes and ol' Slick and I would go out and hunt them. I would pick up a pipe and look in it, and down out the other end would come the skunk. Sometimes Slick would grab and tear it to bits before I could fire a shot. After a day of that, my mom would say, "John, you can't come in the house. You've got to stay out on the porch." She'd wash all my clothes, but even though I had washed and washed and washed I'd still smell like skunk when I went to school.

One day I was out on my uncle's mowing machine with two horses pulling it. The alfalfa was about waist–high and full of pheasants. Old Slick was chasing birds and he got in front of the mowing machine. Before I could stop, his hind leg was caught and the machine darn near severed it. Just a tiny bit of muscle held it together. I put him in my arms, pulled up the sickle, and headed back for the ranch—probably two miles away. I got him to the ranch and some of the hired men helped me sew him back together with a needle and thread, and he recovered just fine. I didn't think he'd ever walk again, but he did.

Our driveway was an easement through a tree farm, about a quarter of a mile long, lined with English walnuts on each side. These were huge trees and all the walnuts that fell in the road belonged to Dad. We had walnut trees in the back yard too. When a nut fell off the tree, Dad taught old Slick to run over there and get it, then bring it back and put it in a bucket. Slick loved that more than catching skunks. He'd lie out there, and look and wait and look and wait, and then BAM, a walnut would hit the ground—and off he'd go. So Slick picked up all the walnuts that fell in the back yard. We would get the rest by putting canvases under the trees and then shaking them. We funneled the canvas into buckets and boxes and picked up the nuts that way.

I also liked to fish whenever I had a chance. The Santa Ana River was a great place for us to catch trout and bullfrogs. We caught quite a few fish in there, most of the time with just a string tied to a stick.

We lived on the same ranch twice. My dad sold it and we moved to Los Angeles. He bought a lot of land and developed it, and we moved back and bought the same darn ranch again. And lived in the same darn house. The first time we lived there we had a dairy with livestock; the second time, we farmed it, raising hay and about 20 acres of black–eyed beans. With less livestock to worry about, I had more time to go hunting and work on my cars.

CHAPTER 3

Gunpowder and Crankshafts

We didn't have many deer in southern California in the 1920s. There were a few around Pomona, but they were so scarce it was a big deal when my neighbor shot a little forkhorn buck. Neighbors walked or drove from around the area to take a look at it.

Cottontail rabbits and jackrabbits were plentiful. A box of 22 long rifle cartridges cost 20 cents. Even when I didn't have money for other revolver cartridges or shotgun shells, I always had enough to buy a box of 22s. I would walk into the southern hills near Pomona, or take a horse or a wagon up there, tie the horses and go walking. My friends and I shot squirrels and rabbits. We saw coyotes around but I never got close enough to shoot one with my 22.

In junior high, I took my dad's old double–barreled shotgun to the school's woodworking shop. My shop teacher showed me what to do and I sanded down the stock and varnished it. It turned out nice for my first try and my dad was proud of the work I'd done.

Back then, a mule deer was the ultimate trophy and I wanted a deer rifle. A guy I knew had a 25–35 Winchester lever action and I traded him a set of Model T connecting rods for that gun. I was rough on Model T Fords, so I always had lots of spare parts around. After I got the Winchester, I hunted with it for several years. I shot a few rabbits with it, but wasn't able to get a deer until I moved to Oregon.

In those days, Western Auto Supply sold a tremendous amount of hop–up material for Model T Fords. I got my first Model T and spent all the money I made on it.

I started buying performance parts, a bigger carburetor and a high–compression head. Then a little later in school, I built up a good Model T race motor. It had overhead valves, a big carburetor, cam, and a crankshaft I had worked over on the school's metal lathe. A friend of mine gave me a set of aluminum connecting rods for race Model T's and I had that fixed up. Art Humphreys and I drove it down to Yuma, Arizona, and back to California.

My first overhead valve setup for my Model T was made by a guy named Roof. He made cylinder heads and I had one of his that had four valves and double pipe rocker arms. Sometimes it would come apart and the little spacers would fly in all directions. So I soldered a bathtub chain to each one so when they would go down the crankcase I could pull them out and put them back in. I got tired of that head and went to the Rajio four–valve system.

Any time something broke, I fixed it. I came to believe that problems weren't problems but opportunities for me to make a bad machine good or a good machine better.

My dad bought some land in Bell, California, outside Los Angeles. I enrolled in high school and tried out for the football team. We won the 1929 city championship with me playing end. I also played baseball and basketball, and ran track. But something happened that year that would change California and America forever. I hardly knew what the stock market was in 1929, but it crashed that year and changed everything. We were on the verge of what historians would come to call the Great Depression.

16

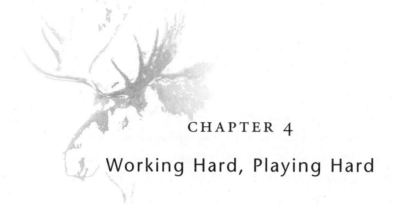

CHAPTER 4

Working Hard, Playing Hard

Dad bought a hotel in Anaheim, invested too much money and lost it when the market crashed and the bottom fell out of the economy. I had to quit high school in my junior year and go to work to help support our family.

I went to the neighborhood Ford garage in Chino and asked them if they would hire me as a clean–up boy. They said they had been looking for someone and so I got the job. I cleaned up after the mechanics and did odd jobs around the dealership, cleaning parts, floors, and cars. But I had a world of experience before that from living on the ranch and working on all the equipment we had on the farm. No one mentioned how much I would be paid. No one talked about that because just having a job was the important thing. I worked a month or two and finally the guy said "John, we like you, so we're going to give you 15 cents an hour." Sounded good to me.

Working for the Ford dealership gave me a lot of opportunity to learn more about mechanics and get involved in racing. I bought cars, fixed them up, and sold them.

There were racetracks in nearly every major city. Huntington Beach had a racetrack out in an old farmer's field. Riverside had another. In Alhambra, there was a track on Jim Jeffrey's ranch. There were five tracks we went to all the time.

After I had worked there a year, the boss and the foreman of the shop got into an argument. The boss fired the foreman. By that time, I was doing mechanic work of all kinds. The boss said "John, do you think you could handle this thing?" I said, "I sure would love to try," so I got the foreman's job.

Life was good for this farm boy. I was working on cars during the day, racing in the evening, and hunting when I had a few hours off.

When we had some time off one day, another kid and I went deer hunting. It was hot, probably 100 degrees. We had a canteen we had packed along, but one of us laid it down on a rock on top of a hill. We walked off and forgot it. When we started getting thirsty, relief was a long way away.

We had walked farther than we should have and there was no water around. My lips were hot and dry, my tongue was like a dry stick clicking around in my mouth, and I felt lightheaded. How had we walked so far from the car? When we finally came upon an old farm tractor sitting in a field, we managed to open the radiator petcock on that thing and get some water out, letting it drain down into our mouths. I wouldn't do it today, but that water sure tasted good after a long hike.

But there was more to keep me entertained in those days. Will Rogers came to the movie house in Pomona a few times and I went to see him three times. Those were Prohibition days and liquor was hard to come by. A few of my buddies and I had met some bootleggers. That was a pastime of many kids our age. Someone would rent a house for five or ten dollars and set up chairs, and everyone would sit

The Ford Garage in Chino, California where John Nosler worked during the Depression.

Readying for race day at the Huntington Beach racetrack. Most of the racers used Model T bodies on the Model A chassis. John's revolutionary counterbalanced Model B crankshaft helped keep his car at the head of the pack.

around an old galvanized washtub with some ice and homebrew stuck in there. It usually cost ten to fifteen cents a bottle.

In the Chino area the Italians raised a lot of grapes and figs. Naturally, some of those grapes turned into wine. I worked on cars for some of the Italians. I'd get acquainted with them and they'd sell me a gallon of wine for a dollar.

I learned early that if I had a project that needed some capital investment bringing in a partner was a good way get the money. Another kid and I owned a 1930 Ford roadster. We stripped the fenders off and worked on it whenever we had a chance. I had a Riley head made by George Riley from Los Angeles. It had two intake valves in the head and used the exhaust valve in the block. Very efficient. It was one of the best racing heads, I think.

In 1932 we bought a new Ford roadster. The V–8 was available but we had so many race parts for the Model A and B engines that we stuck with them. The A and B engines were the same, except that the B's heads had higher compression and the B had a little better camshaft and a heavier crankshaft. The crank looked exactly like that of the Model A's except it was bigger. We

19

thought the B's crankshaft would be great for racing but found out it didn't work well, because they put too much weight on it and it didn't counterbalance. Under high revolutions, it would get wound up too tight and the crankshaft would bend and wipe out the center main.

We had a lot of money invested in that new Model A, had stripped the fenders and windshield off and were ready to race, except we couldn't keep crankshafts in it. My partner had an uncle in Ontario who owned a machine shop and he let us use his tools anytime we wanted to. Boy, did we take advantage of that! We were in his shop one day and I came up with the idea that we had to tack some weights on this crankshaft to counterbalance it. Two weights on the end and in the middle, opposite each other. We road–tested the new crank and that engine purred like a kitten. No more connecting rod trouble. It would do 100 miles an hour easy and I couldn't wait to try it on the track.

We ran it the first time at Long Beach on a one–mile flat, sandy dirt track. The track would get rough because you'd spin sideways going around the corner, shifting and drifting in a cloud of dirt and smoke. I liked working on the engines better than driving, so we chose a friend of ours who really wanted to be a driver.

Each race was 15 to 20 laps. Between 30 and 40 hot–rod Fords and Chevys all running flat out, pedals to the floor. Our '32 Model A with that Model B motor showed those other guys what a balanced engine was capable of. They ate our dust for awhile, going around corners, running the same engines in those cars as the big speedway in L.A. called Ascot. It was good experience for all of us. A few of the drivers I knew went on to race on the bigger tracks, and some went to Indianapolis.

As foreman of the garage, I got to go into Long Beach to a big Ford assembly plant there. All the shop guys got to go visit the plant once a month. They would tell us all the latest things that they had found out on repairing and faster ways to do things and general knowledge. I was so proud of this crankshaft that I'd made that I took it in to them and their engineers ooh–ed and aah–ed and thought balancing was a pretty good idea. They asked if they could keep it there and I said "yes" because it was winter and we weren't racing.

Without my knowledge, they sent the new crankshaft to Detroit and Ford liked it so well that they changed out all the crankshafts in dealer stock. Ford forged them with the weights on. As far as I know I was the first one to take a Model B engine and balance it.

I loved racing, but it was dangerous work. Bob Hawn was one of my good friends. His uncle was a movie actor and owned a chicken ranch in Chino. Bob's cousin, the movie star's son, was absolutely wild about racing. In 1932, V–8s were running their own races and Ford was going all out on them—getting lots of advertising. They were fast. In those days, Indy had two guys in the vehicle—the driver and the mechanic. Bob couldn't get a driving deal so he rode as a mechanic. After ten laps, the car turned over and killed him.

Later, we made a racecar from an old Model T body to get lighter. We were looking for a better front axle than the Model A Ford had. One model had a tubular axle and spindles, so we got one of those from a wrecked car and put that in. It looked awful good but the spindles weren't made as good as we thought they were. A friend of our's was driving that at Huntington Beach. The outside wheel's spindle

For this deer hunt, John and Ralph Julian (right) borrowed Winchester lever–action rifles.

Louise and a friend try their hand with the rifles.

broke, causing the car to spin around. Another car hit him, turned his car over on him and killed him. Another real good buddy of mine lost to racing. That took the wind out of my sails and I quit. I put the roadster back in road condition and tried to stay away from the tracks.

One day, a friend of mine said, "John, I know two French gals you ought to meet." So he took me to Pomona to introduce me. Their names were Louise and Simone. I was taken with Louise.

Her father had been an attorney in France. He joined the war effort, was sent to the front and killed in the first month of the war, leaving a young wife and two daughters (Louise and Simone) behind. The family were wealthy winemakers with a lot of land. Their big three–story house had been opened for servicemen, mostly officer types. Louise's mother got to know a fellow named Mel Booz, a first lieutenant with the U.S. Army.

Her family was mad at Louise's mother because they wanted her to marry into a royal family and she married Mel instead. After the war, Mel found a job as paymaster in the Panama Canal Zone. The new family moved to Panama. When they moved back to the States, they settled in Santa Barbara, California. Mel started working for Pennzoil and became their Credit Manager.

Louise's mother opened a beauty college, teaching young girls how to be beauticians. But she soon grew ill and her doctor told her she had cancer. Mel bought a house in Hollywood and the girls finished high school there while their mother got good medical care. When she passed away, Mel went back to the Canal Zone as paymaster and left one of the beauty colleges to the two girls in Pomona. They were running it when I met them. I was 20 and Louise was 19.

I knew a bootlegger in the neighborhood, so we swung by his place and picked up a few bottles of beer. Louise and I were sitting in the back of the Model A and the other couple was sitting up front. We put the beer on the floor.

I was wearing bell–bottom pants and I must have gotten five bottles of beer under each bell–bottom. The Model A was jigging and bouncing along, and that beer got shook up. Pretty soon one of the caps popped off and blew beer all over my leg, then another one blew and another. I had very wet pants and not much beer left when we got to where we were going.

Louise didn't like to ride in the '32 roadster so I bought a new '33 coupe and we started seeing a lot of each other.

One day I got to go back into the Ford Assembly Plant. One of the managers took me aside. He said Ford wanted young guys like me with an interest in auto mechanics. They were willing to send me to school and after graduation I would be an engineer for Ford Motor Company. I was tempted, but I had met Louise, had a good job, and we wanted to get married. I could see my whole life ahead of me and I didn't see how four years of engineering school fit into it. 🦋

CHAPTER 5

Work, Wedding Rings, and Responsibility

We had our marriage license but no real plan about when to use it. No one spent a lot of money on weddings during the Depression. Some friends of ours wanted to get married in December of 1933 and Louise and I decided we would too.

I knew where the minister lived. We all went down to his house one evening after dark and knocked on his door. His wife answered and said, "No, he's not here. He's down at the movie house." We went down to the theater and told the girl at the counter what we wanted. She said, "Okay, I'll have him paged." We went back to his home and he married us.

The first two months of our married life we lived in a little house in Pomona. Louise drove me to work in Chino, then went to work at her beauty school in Pomona. She had some girls working for her at that time. When she found someone who wanted to buy the business, she sold out and we moved to Chino and got a nice house there.

Being closer to work was a real improvement and I looked for ways to make more money. Whenever a Model A Ford came in with scored brake drums, I chucked them up in my lathe and turned them nice and smooth, making a little bit of extra money that way. I got to be pretty good with the lathe.

Just having a job in those days was reason to celebrate. Very few people had any money. If you had a job, you worked as much as you could. Time off from work was not easy to come by. Your boss couldn't afford to pay you and you couldn't afford to not work. It was two years after we married before I took a day off.

As shop foreman, I was making $90 a month, which was way above average. Louise and I decided we'd like to go to Death Valley. On a two–day national holiday we closed the shop and headed up the ridge route north and into the Mojave Desert.

We stayed in a campground with a little bathhouse because Louise had to have a shower the next morning. The water had to be heated inside the building, then carried outside and up a narrow little ladder, and poured over the person inside. After that we headed out in the car to see the country.

That night we were driving on a lonely, blacktopped road through the valley with very high sagebrush on each side when a herd of cattle came running across the road. I hit the brakes, but I was going too fast and there were too many cows. I plowed into one with the front fender, then the car bounced around and smacked the cow with the back fender.

Driving through Death Valley late at night, John took on a herd of cattle with his Ford. And lost.

Louise with her new car, a 1935 Ford sedan.

We rattled back to Mojave to find one little store open with a dozen people inside, drinking coffee and smoking. The police chief in the room looked at me as I walked in and said, "You must be an auto mechanic." I said I was and asked him how he knew. He said, "Well, you're driving around with only one headlight." So I told him about hitting the cow. "Where at?" he asked. "Oh, about five miles down the road," I replied. "Well, bring it in," he said, "and we'll have a hell of a barbecue." I told him where it was so he could go get it.

A window was broken so I made a cardboard panel to cover it. We were depressed about wrecking the car. We saw Death Valley Scotty's place and tried to enjoy the flowers, but all we could think about was our beautiful car. Gasoline here was 35 cents a gallon. We were used to paying 10 cents and I'd never heard of paying 35 cents a gallon anywhere. So we headed home to Los Angeles and went back to work.

The reality of being married, and being responsible for someone other than me, was beginning to sink in. Louise was expecting our first baby in August. I was 23 and she was 22. Our whole lives were ahead of us and I still had grease under my fingernails.

How was I going to make a place for myself in the world? I had about eight mechanics working under me at that time. I told them, "Any of you guys who like working here need to spend an hour after work selling cars. You guys are going to be salesmen and I'm going to be your sales manager." My group of mechanics put up a pretty doggone good sales organization. In about a year–and–a–half, I put over $1800 into the bank in addition to what I had already put away. I wanted to see if I could buy a Ford agency.

It was time to do something different. Things were going well, but I had moved around so much when I was young, it was hard staying in one place. A part of me still regretted saying no to engineering school and a career at Ford. Having been a Ford man for so long, I naturally went back to Ford when it was time to make a change.

CHAPTER 6

North to Oregon—
A Ford Coupe and Too Much Credit

I was young, but so was Ford Motor Company. I told them I was sorry I had turned down the engineering education and career three years ago, but thought I could handle a Ford agency in a small town. They said they had two openings: one in California and another in Reedsport, Oregon.

I went to Reedsport and looked it over, then talked to the banker in the nearby town of Gardiner and told him what I wanted to do. "I'll help you all I can," he said. He wasn't much older than I was and we got along great. I went back and quit my job, sold my new 1935 Ford to get all the cash I could, and bought a 1929 Ford coupe for $60. We made our plans and packed our things, shipping them north to Reedsport. We were anxious to get settled in our new home.

Our first son, Ron, was born early on August 22, 1936. From Pomona we had about 15 miles to drive to the hospital. Ron was born as soon as we got there.

Our little boy was two months old when we made the move. We packed everything we owned in and on top of our 1929 Ford. Louise, her sister Simone, Ron, and I squeezed inside and drove from Los Angeles to Reedsport, Oregon. We stopped at service stations along the way and used their electricity to warm up milk for the baby.

Today, I own a '29 Ford coupe. It's kind of small for even two people to go very far in, much less three adults and a baby, all riding in that tiny little seat. Of course, we were all skinny then, in the middle of the Great Depression.

I wanted to drive straight through, and not spend any money on motels or restaurants. We bought groceries in stores along the way, putting together our meals and eating on the road. When I grew too tired to drive, we pulled into a campground, set up a tent and went to sleep.

We got to Reedsport and rented a nice apartment. Simone lived with us and was the secretary for the Ford garage. The building is still there. We had a service station out in front then. What was the old agency is now a storage area. On one of the bricks up above, it says 1936 on it. We did pretty well at first. I know I would have made it if the labor union had not come in.

Ford had a program where they worked with a credit company to help people buy cars. Some of the reasonably priced cars could be bought at $25 down and $25 per month; the more expensive models cost $50 a month.

The only problem in those days was that when the dealer sold the loan to a credit company the dealer was still responsible for it. Not today. If the customer can't pay, the credit company owns it. If a customer brought the car back to me because he

Before he moved north to Oregon, John sold his 1935 Ford and purchased a '29 Coupe (above) for $60.00

Racing on sand—minus fenders, top and windshield—John rolled this 1929 Ford and walked away from the accident. Later on, he put it back in road condition and slowed down a bit.

couldn't pay, I had to pay off the credit company immediately—not tomorrow, but right then.

I had sold over a hundred cars by the time the unions organized in Reedsport. The lumber workers wanted a union and got organized. And a union was the last thing the sawmill owners wanted. Sawmills were only keeping the doors open to keep their people working. When the unions organized, all the sawmills just turned out the lights and locked the doors. In small towns up and down the coast, people quit buying lumber. Stacks of boards lay rotting in the mill yards, because demand had died. And when the mills closed, all the cars I had sold started coming back.

I paid all the bills I could and took my Ford cars and trucks over to Eugene to try to sell them there. I'd put them up for half of what they were worth and still couldn't sell near enough to do us any good. The Depression was still on and the lumber layoff ricocheted. Everyone was scared to death and no one knew what to do. They sure weren't buying cars. The people that brought them back were all sorry they couldn't pay for them, even at $25 a month. I was sorry too.

I called a friend of mine in southern California whose dad had a bit of money and said, "Why don't you zoom up here and take over my agency? You can have it lock, stock and barrel. All you'll have to do is pay a few bills." He took it and we headed to Ashland, Oregon, and a new start.

I was looking forward to the move for another reason. I had heard that Ashland was in the middle of good deer country and I hoped to do more hunting. 🦌

CHAPTER 7

TRUCKING AND TARGET SHOOTING

I put a down payment on a 1937 Ford truck chassis we had sitting on the showroom floor in Reedsport, and drove it to Ashland. My brother and cousin were living there, and I thought I'd be able to make some money with it. My cousin and I planned to bring fruits and vegetables in from California when Oregon farmers would freeze out, and sell our produce to the stores. We called our company Nosler Produce.

In those days San Francisco had a produce consignment market. A packing house would consign crates of lettuce, celery, and potatoes and sell them to the highest bidder. We started by buying our produce at the farmers' markets in Sacramento and Stockton and sold it in Oregon.

When my cousin grew bored with trucking and wanted to do something else, I bought out his interest. I increased sales and took on more stores, then decided I needed a bigger truck.

At that time I kept a buyer in the San Francisco market. I told him to look around for a bigger truck when he didn't have anything else to do. He heard about a guy named Peterman who was beginning to build trucks for the highway.

I bought the first or second Peterbilt with trailer ever made. I could haul 20 tons with it, while the most the Fords could haul was 7–8 tons. I'd go down with a driver, buy a load, and come back to Oregon.

That Peterbilt Cummins diesel got 5 miles to the gallon, sometimes 7, about the same as the Ford was getting, but diesel was only 5 cents a gallon where gasoline cost 23 cents. When we were going to L.A., we could buy diesel at 3 cents a gallon. Diesel was a drug on the market at the time; the refiners had to make it to get gasoline so they'd dump it off. I became very successful and ended up with several

Ready for the road. In 1939, the Nosler Produce fleet was growing.
Don Brace (left), Marion Mann, John and Ron Nosler.

John Nosler and
Don Brace pose
with a Peterbilt.

John riding Gypsy near
Ashland, Oregon

Loaded up and ready to roll down the
highway to California. This truck was one
of the first Peterbilts ever made.

Peterbilts. Had one in every place. With good people working for me, I had time to hunt.

There was a lot of interest in shooting in those days. If you were into target shooting as I was, you found out pretty soon that to compete you needed to shoot fine–tuned, match–grade ammunition. This simply was not available during the war years and immediately afterward. Reloading was starting to catch on as people realized they could make their own custom loads, tailored to fit their rifles and handguns. They could also save a little money by loading their own.

Fred Huntington, Joyce Hornady, Bruce Hodgdon, the Speers, and others like them were traveling around the country, putting on ammunition reloading seminars at police stations, gun clubs, sporting goods stores, schools, and anywhere else they could find shooters to listen.

I started competitive shooting very early in Ashland with the Ashland Gun Club. At first, I was gone an awful lot with business but in the winter I managed to get home on Tuesday nights. We made a deal with the National Guard Armory to start a shooting club in their basement.

I bought quarter–inch plate in five–by–ten–foot sheets and we set them up at an angle to deflect bullets into wooden mangers filled with sawdust. The bullet would strike the target, hit that quarter–inch plate and ricochet down into the sawdust. We never had a safety problem but sometimes had to replace the quarter–inch plate after the National Guard would sneak in and shoot the hell out of our range with their 30–06 full metal jacket bullets.

We had ten very small targets to shoot at 50 feet. I would lay my shooting mat down, wrap my forearm in the sling and start from prone. There was a time limit in which to fire. Before giving the signal to fire, the range officer would look up and down the line. "Ready on the left," he'd yell. "Ready on the right. When satisfied, "Commence firing." There'd be 10 or 15 of us lying down there and shooting at any one time. The rule was ten shots at each target with one "sighter" target you could come back to any time you wanted. Then you'd score them. A good score was between 87 and 90.

Everyone would get 100 when prone and sitting. Kneeling was a little harder. Some knelt, sitting on their foot in a vertical position. More limber shooters would sit on their foot in a horizontal position. If you could lay your foot down and sit on it, your body could be used as a steady shooting platform. If you could only sit on your heel with your toe on the ground, you weren't as steady. Some of the best marksmen were our female shooters.

We had matches in Oregon with Medford or Grants Pass or in Yreka, California. Sometimes we held "postal" matches with clubs from Alaska and elsewhere in the states. You'd have all their addresses and write them that you'd be open on such and such a time and would like to shoot, then mail the targets and score them, and prizes would be awarded.

In the summertime we'd shoot outdoors, prone and standing, sometimes kneeling, sometimes sitting. We would start out at 100 yards then we'd often shoot, all standing, at 200 yards with the big rifles. For shorter distances, we used 22s but for 200–yard competitions we used whichever rifle we wanted. The National Rifle Association (NRA) had a match that was 200 yards prone and offhand. The X–ring was about 3 inches or so. Prone, you'd get it dead center all the time, but offhand

A few of the medals John won in target shooting competitions in Ashland, Oregon.

it was very tough. Especially, if there was a little wind. At the 100–yard shoots in Medford, they'd be through shooting and there'd be a fly or a grasshopper on the target in the field and they'd try to hit it.

The NRA classified shooters according to their ability. Master Rifleman was best, Expert Rifleman was next best, and so forth. I shot Expert most often and Master for awhile.

I used the 7 mm Magnum quite a bit. I actually developed a 7 mm Magnum long before Remington did. In fact, they were so close that trimming the neck on the case about .040, I believe you could shoot one of my old rounds in a Remington chamber. Later I used it to take moose, elk, deer, Rocky Mountain goats, and black bears. It was flat–shooting and accurate.

I became interested in making chamber reamers. I went down to San Diego and met a guy who was making them, and spent some time with him. He taught me all that he had learned so I began to make and sell a few.

We shot indoors in the basement of the Ashland National Guard building once a week in the winter. All indoor shooting was at 50 feet—prone, sitting, kneeling, and off–hand. All rifles were match grade Winchester Model 52s or Remington 37s. Everyone used match ammo. Winchester made the 22 Easy Xs and most of us chose them.

I've always enjoyed inventing. I got the idea that I could build a multi–stage rifle in order to gain higher velocity. So I worked up an experimental model based on a Model 70 action, feeding in three charges of gunpowder in stages. I drilled ports on each side of the barrel and welded on canisters that would accept extra charges of powder in brass cases. Each canister was sealed with a threaded plug.

The shooter would load a factory round into the chamber. When fired, the bullet passed down the barrel. As the bullet passed each port, an additional charge of 60 to 100 grains of powder would ignite, giving the bullet a boost from each port. The rifle belched flame and smoke like a dragon. I experimented with penetration of sheets of steel, stacking them side by side. I finally blew the thing to smithereens. I tried several different powders and one day used a fast–burning pistol powder that blew the screws right out of the ports. I never found them.

I imagine it would have kicked like three mules, but I never found out. I only shot that one on a tripod with a *long* string. I decided it was time my old Model 70 went back to being a hunting rifle, so I put a new barrel on it and used it many more years.

Louise became my bookkeeper. She had a good head for business and helped me put money in the bank with those trucks. I was so proud of the way she helped me that I bought her a new 1938 Ford car. One day I was headed home through Central Oregon with one of my drivers in one of our Ford trucks. We were crossing the river north of Terrebonne when the engine threw a rod and went to rattling something fierce. We managed to pull it over. I found a phone and called Louise, asking her if she would mind bringing her new car from Ashland to take us home.

By the time she showed up, we had the old engine out of that truck. In a few hours, we had the motor out of Louise's car and were headed for home, towing the little Ford behind us.

I never broke a bone except when I was in the trucking business. One day while unloading an open trailer full of oranges in crates, I fell chest-down on one of the posts sticking up above the sideboards. I broke my clavicle and it was very painful.

I had to go to San Francisco that night to buy produce for the next day's delivery. I told the kid riding with me to phone a doctor I knew in Red Bluff, tell him what the situation was, and ask him to get me some pain pills. He did and we went to the drug store and picked up the prescription. I bought my 20 tons of produce, loaded it up (of course, I had guys do the loading that time) but I never missed a beat. It was the most painful thing I ever felt and it bothered me for a long time.

Many of Ashland's businessmen belonged to the Elks Club. Old Doc Haines was a good friend of mine and a former World War I doctor. Doc Haines, the druggist, the guy who had the Ford Agency, and I were all good friends and went up to the Elks Club and shot craps at night. I won some pretty good money from old Doc Haines one night and talked him into removing my appendix, because I was afraid I'd get way out in California and my appendix would break.

I shot my first deer east of Ashland, off the Green Springs Road between Ashland and Klamath Falls. That's still a good deer area. We hunted blacktails there. They were the sneaking–est, hiding–est animals you ever saw. If you could get by the poison oak and rattlesnakes, there were a lot of deer. I found a bunch of them.

We made the run over the mountain to Klamath Falls, driving those trucks back and forth every week. During the season, I'd carry a 30–30 with me and bring home a deer. When I got a little better organized, I started hunting in Eastern Oregon.

I left Louise at home when I was on the road with the trucks or out hunting. She ran the business very well because she knew everything I did. We had few difficulties with employees because all our drivers were like family. So I was able to do a lot of hunting around the country. I used to go around Mendocino County every year in California and shoot two blacktails. Then I would go down into Modoc and hunt mule deer. In Oregon, I roamed around the Steens and Trout Creek Mountains for mule deer and hunted near Ashland for blacktails.

Deer were plentiful and I was getting pretty good at deer hunting, so I thought I would try my hand at elk and maybe hunt for moose some day. This would change my life. 🦌

CHAPTER 8

Elk, Ammunition, and Amigos

There weren't many elk in Oregon when I was young, but they are everywhere now. When I first started hunting in British Columbia up and down the coast range, I never saw elk. Today there are many in Canada, Alaska, and many places in Oregon where we never would have expected to see elk 40 years ago.

Elk had been thinned out by the early settlers and were found only in the high mountains. We never saw any elk in desert areas where you can find them today. We did hunt in mountain forests and shot some fine bulls, but only in the higher elevations.

I killed my first bull in eastern Oregon near Burns in the Silvies River area soon after I moved to Ashland. One of my employees went along and we brought Con Fury who worked for the Soil Conservation Service in Spokane. Con was a great big guy, a football player who had played guard for Oregon State when they went to the Rose Bowl.

We camped about a mile from where we were going to hunt up on a ridge and damn near froze to death. We had two tents: one for gear and one we slept in. Folding cots allowed the air to circulate beneath us and the sleeping bags we had were only suitable for summertime backyard campouts, not for elk season.

So we slept in our clothes, piled more clothes on top of our bags and crowded all together in one little tent. I set up a coal oil stove and tried to make a chimney for the fumes to escape. I guess it worked because I'm still alive.

Before going elk hunting that first time, I talked to a lot of old–timers to find out how. They said to follow a ridge down until I came to a break. The elk would cross on those breaks.

On opening day, the other guys left half an hour before me, early in the morning. They were going to set up in a saddle, build a fire and wait for the elk to come through. I was headed their way when I heard some shooting, and here came this five–point bull elk running straight at me. He stopped about 30 yards out and looked at me. It took one shot. The bullet hit him in the neck and he dropped.

One of my truck drivers brought an old surplus 30–40 Krag bolt–action like those used in the Spanish–American War. We had fixed it up with a new stock and better sights and converted it into a sporter. The ammunition was very poor. He got into a herd of elk, hit three different animals, and never knocked one of them down.

One of John's early elk camps in Oregon's Silvies Mountans. "On opening day, the other guys left half an hour before me, early in the morning. They were going to set up in a saddle, build a fire and wait for the elk to come through. I was headed their way when I heard some shooting, and here came this five–point bull elk..." ~ John Nosler

We came up to where he had shot and read the story in the snow. We started following our partner because his tracks trailed the elk and we could see the blood trail. Though we followed him for a long time, we never did catch up with the elk. But the old 30–40 Krag shot so slow and ammunition was so poorly loaded back then, that the bullets never even expanded.

For deer, we hunted in the Steens Mountains. It was great, wide–open country with the best deer habitat I ever found—deep canyons, good cover, enough water, and escape habitat. We became friends with many ranchers in the area and looked forward to deer and pronghorn seasons.

Ralph Waterman (left), Ron Nosler, John, unidentified soldier, and Con Fury with the fruits of a deer hunt in Southeast Oregon in 1944.

After a few years, I got better at setting up my hunting camps. I had a 16 x 20-foot tent, with 5-foot-high walls, a cook stove, and a warm-up stove. I enjoyed taking large groups out with me.

Con Fury brought a friend of his named Bill Stew who had come from Africa and worked for the English government in their African colonies at an earlier period, surveying mineral deposits. He came to know Africa pretty well.

John's Model A Ford that served as his wartime deer hunting rig.

Bob Van Vleet with a nice mule deer from the Steens Mountains.

Stew and I shot some deer together and a number of elk. One day he said, "John, if you would like to make a lot of money, you and I'll go to Africa and we'll buy a truck on one side. I know how to get through from one side of Africa to the other with a truck. Elephants are in there by the thousands. We'll shoot elephants and load the tusks in the truck and we'll get so damn many tusks we'll have to go several times to the depot to deposit our ivory." It was fun to think about but ridiculous to go, because I had a family and a business that had taken a lot of work to build. But I thought, even though I can't go to Africa, I can probably swing a hunt for moose.

CHAPTER 9

Moose, a Mountie,
and John Henderson

By 1941, the trucking business was doing well for us and I decided to reward myself with a trip to British Columbia. My buddies, Marion Mann (one of my employees) and Walt Remmy, both good hunters and sportsmen, jumped at the chance to hunt moose with me. None of us had gone after moose before but we talked about it and asked ourselves, "How hard can it be? Sure, moose are larger than deer and elk, but that makes them better targets." Easier to hit, yes, but harder to bring down. I loaded the ammunition for us all, using the best bullets and powders available at that time.

Roads from Vancouver, B.C., north into the remote area of British Columbia where we wanted to hunt were not the expressways we drive today. Air travel was expensive, so we loaded up my 1940 gunmetal gray Ford pickup and took to the unpaved byways. Though we got an early start, by the time we crossed the Canadian border, we'd been driving for 12 hours. Detours to find service stations to feed the pickup's gas–guzzling flathead V–8 added miles to our journey.

When a weather–beaten sign announced the town of Williams Lake, Marion wanted to wet his whistle and Walt suggested finding a guide. Choices of where to try our luck were limited to a tavern and an old barn that had been converted into a hotel. A Mountie sitting at the tavern's counter seemed a good bet for information on where we might find someone to show us the ropes. He looked over the truck and gear piled in the back. "If you can handle rough country," he said, "take the trail west, cross over the Frasier River, and head for the mountains in the coast range. The track's so poor you'll lose it sometimes, but try to go a couple hundred miles on it.

You'll see Indians from time to time. They ought to be able to tell you where to find game."

This road was, if possible, worse than any of the ones we'd driven to get here. Several times we had to backtrack when it became clear the path we were on was going nowhere. We got so tired from fighting the ruts and the holes and the mud that we finally stopped, set up the canvas tent by flashlight, and tunneled into our sleeping bags. Right in the middle of the road.

Five hours later according to the tired hands of my wristwatch, crisp daylight crept through the front flap of the tent. I opened my eyes. Walt and Marion were still snoring to beat the band. I wiggled my sleeping bag over to the tent flap and peered outside. The old Indian trail next to us had few tracks of cars. The truck's gas tank was less than half full. It didn't seem likely we'd be rescued if we ran out of fuel or broke an axle. As I wondered how we were ever going to get back to civilization (and how we'd hold our heads up if we came back empty–handed), I heard what sounded like a rooster crowing. Impossible, I thought. We were way back in the dark

Johnny Henderson readies a pack horse to carry out a mountain goat at the end of a successful day.

Canadian woods. Then the sound came again. Only a rooster made such a raucous noise so early in the morning. There must be a farm nearby.

I let out a yell and woke my buddies. We threw our gear into the back of the pickup, and drove in the direction of the rooster's yodels. As the trees thinned out, we saw a large spread. The rancher sold us fuel and had his cook give us breakfast. They did not depend on the uncertain roads we had navigated but brought supplies in by boat from the coast. After his second cup of coffee, Walt got down to business. "Where can we hunt?" The rancher told us about an Indian man and his wife who had a small spread a few miles to the west. They were sure he would be willing to guide us. We thanked them and took to the road again.

A collie greeted us at the entrance to John Henderson's place. Bounce put up quite a fuss, until John Henderson came out of the cabin. His appearance made it clear he lived off the land. He wore a flannel cap, wool shirt, and homespun leggings. After some dickering, he agreed to rent us the older cabin on his land. John's father had built this one and John built the newer cabin himself, cutting

Stopping for lunch on the way to British Columbia in the mid–1940s

Headed for home with a big moose head tied on the back.

down pine trees and using an adze to make boards out of the logs. The cabins looked primitive to us, but were well crafted and kept out the rain and wind.

John's wife, Edith, was quite a gal. She had grown up in Idaho and was educated. Other Indians in the area employed her to read their mail and help them with business affairs. She was also a good cook. She had a big garden and stored her produce in a cellar for use in the winter.

John's entire income came from shooting squirrels with a 22 rifle and 22 short ammunition and trapping lynx, marten, and beaver. John and Edith traded garden produce and cured furs to exchange for smoked salmon and deer meat to supplement their groceries. She cooked an awful lot of moose and deer meat for us over the years. Every time we visited them after that, we'd bring boxes of fresh fruit and vegetables with us.

Catalogs from two mail order houses in Canada (similar to Montgomery Ward and Sears) were stacked on a plank table near the fireplace. Barter was used more than cash in the backwoods. John admitted he'd ordered the hand pump mounted on the kitchen sink and the cabin's windows through the mail, but said he'd traded for a lot of it and made everything else himself. He introduced us to the postmaster and his wife who lived nearby. The postmaster was blind and depended on his wife to sort the mail, but he kept all the postage rates in his head.

John was a bit shy (especially when he heard we'd been talking to a Canadian policeman) until we got to know him. He'd been drafted and seen combat in France in World War I. When the soldiers came back to Canada after the war, he was so eager to get home he jumped off the ship a mile from port, swam ashore, and disappeared into the woods. For years, he was afraid to go back into town because he thought a Mountie might arrest him for going AWOL.

Walt Remmy carried a Model 91 Winchester lever action 348. It was a terrific gun. I loaded 250–grain bullets for him that would knock a moose down much better than my rifle. I could get a moose at long range though, and he couldn't touch them. We all killed our moose on that first visit and began to plan next year's trip

We hunted moose, goats, bighorn sheep, and deer with John Henderson seven or eight times over the next few years. Each time John took us into a different part of the country with the words, "White man never been here before."

In the late 1940s, we took the first motorboat ride on Tatlayoko Lake. I don't think there was ever another boat on that lake except for Indian canoes. The road to it was, impossible as that seemed, even worse than the one that had led us to John.

The Indians made a practice of setting trees on fire as a way to improve moose habitat. If we hunted an area and found little game, John said, "Trees no good. We burn this area and get willows going so moose come in." Burning down the larger pine and spruce trees let air and sunlight onto the ground, encouraging the growth of more browse. I finally gave John a talking–to: "You're burning up a hell of a lot of pretty darn good trees." When I told him how much those trees were worth, he had a hard time believing me but he didn't set as many fires after that.

After dark we'd sit around the campfire wherever we stopped hunting for the night, listening to John's stories, which he said had been passed down in his family for generations. "The first moose wandered into our land long time ago." (There was no telling if this meant fifty years or fifty centuries.) "Indians had never seen one before. They held big powwow to decide what to do. No one had ever killed an animal that big. So the people surrounded it and finally killed it with arrows and spears. They butchered it and everyone sat around looking at the meat, but no one wanted to try it. Finally, one brave Indian said he would eat some. When he ate, he found it was good. Then everybody else ate."

Another of John's favorite stories told of territorial disputes between tribes. "A long time ago, the Big Indians tried to take our land. They came into our villages and burned them, and killed our women. We fought them and fought them until they went away and left us alone." John couldn't say how big the "Big Indians" were, just that they were from another area of the forest.

John's storytelling was not confined to distant times. He told of one hunting trip where the tables were turned and a grizzly began to chase *him*. He escaped by running into a small cave he knew of. The grizzly stayed outside the entrance for several days before deciding to look for easier pickings elsewhere, allowing John to escape—hungry as a bear after a long winter's nap.

1941 marked the end of the Great Depression, though we didn't know it at the time, and the beginning of World War II as far as the United States was concerned. It was a turning point in our country's history, and one in my life as well. 🌾

CHAPTER 10

Gas Rationing,
Lever Guns, and Leverage

Ron Nosler and a neighborhood friend in front of
John's wartime hunting rig, a Model A Ford.

December 7, 1941, dawned like any other Sunday but Japanese Zeros, flying out of the sun over Pearl Harbor, made that morning a day that our country and the world would never forget. December 8, 1941, was a Monday like no other Monday that America had ever seen before. Suddenly we were a people with a purpose, a country at war. More young American boys enlisted in the Army, Navy, Air Force, Marines, and Coast Guard on December 8 than any other single day in American history.

Young men, including a lot of my good friends, went off to fight for our country's freedom. Many of them died far across the sea and paid the ultimate price in defense of liberty and self–determination.

In 1941, I was 28 and talked to Louise about going to war, but she pointed out that there were people depending on me here at home. Not only my family, but my employees and their families. She was right, of course.

On the home front, we worked for the war effort however we could—conserving gasoline, tires, metals, hams, bacons, whiskey, wool, and nylon so that our boys could have the best equipment and clothing. We never doubted our cause, even during the darkest days of the war. There was never any doubt that we were working to make our country safe and this world a better place.

During World War II, the government issued gas ration stamps. A person could only buy so much gasoline at any one time. Since you needed gas to go anywhere, most people didn't go hunting during the war.

Business leaders in towns formed "boards" to issue permits to buy tires, gas cards, and whatever else was needed to keep things moving. Trucks that were hauling important goods would get everything they needed to keep them rolling. Repair parts for our trucks were not of the best quality. Tires were very bad because substitutes for rubber were being tried. I was fortunate in that I was able to purchase a number of good tires and store them for use on our trucks.

I decided to repair a Model A Ford coupe and leave it parked to accumulate gas stamps. The longer I let it sit, the more stamps I had. Each gas stamp was good for five gallons per month. When I had saved enough gas stamps, I'd be able to go hunting.

For tires, I would look around for old used Ford rubber ones and I found enough to last me. Later–model car tires were nearly impossible to find. No new guns were available but some could be found in small stores in out–of–the–way places. Shotgun shells could sometimes be found in small towns. My business required me to use large trucks that traveled up and down the West Coast. I told the drivers to stop at all small hardware stores, looking for shotgun shells. I had plenty of shotgun shells, though some were very old. I did get to hunt for ducks, geese, and pheasants during the war, stocking our refrigerator with fresh meat.

When we had enough gas coupons, we took a trip to the Hart Mountain Antelope Refuge that had been closed to hunting for years. They opened it for deer hunting only. Three of us loaded up the Model A Ford and a small trailer. Wardens met us at the entrance. They told us to camp outside the refuge and walk up to the hunting area. We set up our camp in an old CCC (Civilian Conservation Corps) facility. Numerous rattlesnakes kept things interesting. If we had not brought folding cots to sleep on, we would have had snakes in our blankets. It would have been suicide to sleep on the ground. Not one of us got up in the night, there were so many snakes on the ground.

Next morning we were up early and ready to climb. At the entrance trail we met about ten other hunters. One of them had a doe tag. The rest had buck tags. We all began to climb. Soon we spotted a mule deer doe. One of the fellows shot it. "There's your deer," he told the man with the doe permit. "Go tag it."

The man with the doe tag said, "It's not my deer. You shot it, so you tag it." The guy who shot the deer said he had a buck tag and didn't want to put it on a doe. He must have thought he was doing the other man a favor by shooting his deer. We all convinced the shooter that he'd better put his buck tag on that doe. If you hunt long enough, you'll meet all kinds of people.

John, taking little Ron for a ride.

John feeding a pet blacktail doe near Ashland, Oregon

On top of Hart Mountain we saw antelope everywhere. Big deer with good racks were visible a long way out. We spent the day looking things over. Refuge personnel said we would be able to drive in the next day to aid in removal of downed deer.

We drove the old Ford up. It was a hard pull but with some helping to push in a bad spot we made it. We put up our tent near a spring and were ready to hunt. The deer had not been hunted and it was easy to get within rifle range.

The game warden found a dead doe not far from our camp and asked us if we had shot it. We told the warden about the fellow who shot the doe when we were walking up the first day. I would have bet it was the same person's deer. Anyone who shoots deer just to see them die should not be allowed to hunt.

On that hunt I shot a very nice four–point with my hand–loaded 30–06. All three of us shot big bucks. I was using 150–grain bullets made by prisoners in San Quentin for Western Tool and Copper Works. I don't know how the inmates managed to be in the bullet business, but they sold their bullets before the war in large numbers. Their bullets were hollow points, made from copper tubing.

They were pretty good bullets compared to what was then available, but I knew there was a lot of room for improvement. I figured someone would build a better bullet before long.

Once I took some friends on an antelope hunt. I was carrying a lever–action 30–30 at the time. We kicked up a herd of pronghorns and I fired, worked the action, and it jammed. I went back to the truck, picked up my 348 and went hunting again. I should have been using the 348 anyway. I thought that Model 71, chambered in a 348 Winchester, was one of the best handling rifles ever built.

I came up on another buck at 250 yards and shot it with a 150–grain bullet. The buck went down. Upon closer inspection, I found the bullet had struck the animal in the neck, but did not penetrate. From that point on, I always used a 200– or 250–grain bullet when I shot my 348 for the penetration the heavier bullets produced.

Back at camp that evening, I started working on the lever gun to see why it had jammed. I found that the round I was trying to chamber was a 32–caliber bullet. Good thing I couldn't chamber it, because I would've blown up the gun and myself too.

We worked hard during the war years and did without. Though the fight was on other continents, we never forgot that we were a part of the war effort—that our boys were in harm's way in defense of our freedom.

During the war I sold to, and hauled produce for, the government. Our main routes were to Camp White in Medford and the Marine barracks in Klamath Falls, Oregon. Sometimes we hauled produce to the Japanese internment camp in Tulelake, California.

After a few years, veterans began to return from the war. These Marines had a lot of experience in procurement. I would send a driver over with a truckload of fruits and vegetables or meats. Later, the Marines told us they didn't want us to unload at the warehouse, but in a truck on such and such a road. "Security reasons," they said. They said we would see the truck sitting on such and such a road and we should just unload into it. So we did that for a while.

One day I got a visit from the FBI who asked, "Were you unloading trucks out in other places beside the Marine warehouse?" "Yeah," I said, "they told us to take it there instead." We hauled an awful lot of fancy bacon and ham for them, the best that you could get anyplace. We later had to testify against a few of these Marines because they were selling it on the black market. The butcher markets just couldn't get that kind of quality very often, I guess, and a few of them were willing to buy it to have something to sell. The government really wanted to help those Marines, returning from the war. And some of the guys wanted to help themselves.

My son Bob, who is now the president of Nosler, Inc., was born April 21, 1946. Louise and I had spent the day driving around and knew that he could arrive anytime so we went to the theater that night in Ashland. We were watching the movie and Louise said, "I'm getting awfully ready. I think we had better get out of here." We had people on each side of us so I jumped up and announced that my wife was going to have a baby, and did we ever have plenty of room to get out! We rushed to the hospital and made it just in time to welcome young Bob into the world.

From the time he was young, Bob showed an intense interest in sports and the outdoors. From an early age he was my constant companion.

A lot of opportunities come along when you are working hard to get ahead. Some are blind paths that take you to a dead end and some are roads that can lead to riches. I wasn't an expert on metals at the time, but I had an inkling that tungsten might be important in the future. I decided to find out what the experts thought.

Louise's uncle was the head of a firm called Booz, Allen and Hamilton with offices all over the country. We went down to L.A. to visit and I talked to Mel Booz, Louise's stepfather.

At that time, I was hauling from California and Arizona into Oregon and Idaho, selling to the stores. I found a fellow who had some tungsten mines out of Ashland. He would dig this stuff up and check the quality and we would load that in my trucks and haul it down to a refinery in California. I did it quite a bit and he wasn't paying me very well, so I said, "What can I take for some of my expenses?" He wanted me to take interest in the mines but I was a little leery about it. So I told Mel, "Ask your brother what the tungsten relationship might be to the economy in the future."

We went to his brother's office. They recommended I get out of the tungsten business because it was an excellent commodity in time of war but not of much value in peacetime.

Tungsten turned out to be quite valuable during war and peace. Come to think of it, I have paid a lot of consultants over the years to tell me lots of things that turned out not to be true.

I was to learn more about metals in the years to come and my most valuable lesson in metallurgy came in a willow patch in a Canadian swamp, facing a bull moose.

CHAPTER 11

Penetration and Expansion—
The Need for a Better Bullet

I had been looking forward to my next hunt in British Columbia, loading bullets for myself and my companions, and going over the gear list. Now that the war was over, there were a lot of servicemen coming out of the military. Many of these men had traveled around the world, finding adventure and action in places like Guadalcanal, Midway, Normandy, and Tripoli. Civilian life was too calm for many of them now.

Their restlessness led to a resurgence of interest in hunting and shooting. Rifle and shotgun makers were re–tooling, turning out sporting guns instead of military arms. Ammunition suppliers were manufacturing hunting bullets.

America was infused with a can–do attitude. The Great Depression was over, World War II was behind us, and Americans were going and doing like never before.

In 1946, I was shooting a Model 70 Winchester chambered for a 300 H&H Magnum using 180–grain bullets. I loved the way this rifle would shoot at long range. It was accurate and it killed, well, most of the time. The problem was that the bullets expanded too much on heavy game. Bullets shot at such high velocity sometimes flattened out like a pancake and seldom penetrated to the vitals. I learned not to shoot moose in the shoulder with the bullets available. They would overexpand and not penetrate.

Moose wade out to feed in the water and then come out and roll in the dirt. This leaves a heavy coat of clay stuck to them. I soon learned to pass up shots at moose wearing this clay armor. Life was different in the 1940s. In many places at that time, a hunter could legally shoot an animal for another hunter. I think party hunting is still legal in some areas. A hunter was allowed one moose for the year. As long as the moose was tagged, it was legal. That season I shot three moose: one for me, one for Johnny Henderson, and one for the Post Office. Walt and Marion each killed one.

Near the end of the trip, Johnny and I walked up on a big bull in a willow swale. When I saw him, I was too damn close. Behind a screen of willows the big moose stood broadside. His polished antlers gleamed and his body was black with caked mud. I heard the rasp of his breath and smelled the marsh and sweat caked on his body. I'd be gored on his antlers if he decided to charge. I snicked the safety to "fire" on my Winchester Model 70 300 H&H Magnum and snugged the butt against my shoulder.

I settled the crosshair in the pocket behind his front leg and took the slack out of the trigger. I squeezed, rocked with the recoil and cycled the bolt. The bull stepped forward and turned his head in my direction, so I shot him again. He didn't stagger or fall or bellow and charge. Instead, he turned away and started, at a trot, into the trees. I hit him again, then again and saw him stumble at the impact of the fourth bullet.

I reloaded as I followed in his tracks. I knew my bullets had hit him, but it would take several more shots to do the job. The bull was quartering away when I fired again. I stood and fired, worked the bolt and fired. When the bull was finally on the ground, I stepped close, approaching from behind, ready to shoot again if need be.

My friend and guide, Johnny Henderson, helped me with the skinning and we counted the holes, finding that my bullets had struck hard, but splattered on the mud-caked shoulder. My 300 H&H had sent its bullet at such high speed that the thin copper jacket couldn't contain the soft lead core. Though I was shooting from close range, most of my shots didn't even penetrate to the vitals. My new, high-powered rifle was *too* powerful to kill a moose with the bullets available to hunters in the 1940s.

I knew I was a good shot, and had a drawer full of shooting medals back home to prove it. But for a few minutes in that willow swale, standing close enough to the moose to smell his breath, I had to wonder why my shots didn't produce the desired effect. But when we skinned him out, I found that every one of my shots had hit where I had aimed.

My gun was the latest in high–velocity rifles and I was using the best bullets available, but most of them had disintegrated just under the hide. It became clear to me that the bullet hadn't been invented that was good enough to use in a high–velocity rifle.

But over–expansion was only one of the problems. Some bullets penetrated but didn't kill cleanly. On one hunt in British Columbia, I came upon a bull and a cow feeding together. The cow was between the bull and me, so I came in from a different angle so I could shoot the bull without hitting the cow. A stick cracked

Caked in dried mud and sweat, a moose's armor could stop bullets fired from high velocity rifles. Returning home after one hunt, John put his energy toward building a better bullet. The result was the Nosler Partition, a bullet that married penetration with controlled expansion. The revolutionary new design has become the standard by which all hunting bullets are judged.

under my boot and the bull turned to face me, giving me a frontal shot. I took it, hitting him in the chest. The bullet traveled all the way through the animal and exited from the right hindquarter. Today's bullets would have dropped that animal right now. I had to track that old moose for four hours before I caught up and finished him off. I wanted a better bullet.

The day before we were to leave I went hunting again. Sure enough I walked out and stumbled onto a nice bull right away. I did the same darn thing to him. I put two shots in the shoulder and could see that wasn't working so shot him in the belly, and the bullet fragmented so bad in his internal organs that he just keeled right over.

All the way home I was disappointed. Either I had to go back to hunting with my old 30–40 Krag and 30–30 Winchester, or find a better bullet. The next time I was in San Francisco, I visited all the big sporting goods stores to see what they had in 7 mm Magnum or 300 Mag 180–grain bullets. I found some 220–grain ammunition loaded that Winchester claimed made a good African bullet. So I tried those out. They did a better job because the velocity was way down. I don't think they were traveling over 2500 feet per second. I did get one or two through the shoulder on a moose, but it still wasn't the best combination.

The old truck garage that John converted into his first bullet plant in Ashland, Oregon. The very first Partition bullets were built in this building.

Walt Remmy took a 348 Winchester up with him the next trip. He was using the 250–grain, and having great success; he could blow over a moose with that baby right now. The shoulder was the place to hit them with that thing. I had a little experience with that cartridge myself because I owned a 348 and had shot elk with it, but it wasn't the flat–shooting, long–range rifle that the 300 H&H Magnum was.

Surely, I reasoned, there was an answer out there, a way to marry the qualities of penetration and expansion. I just had to keep searching until I found it.

CHAPTER 12

Partitions on a Pie Plate

John and young Ron Nosler on vacation in California.

After I returned to Ashland, I kept thinking about the poor performance that my loads had given on moose. I decided it wasn't the rifle's fault. It was the bullet design that was the problem.

One day I was scribbling on a pad of paper, drawing bullet shapes. I was thinking that I needed penetration and I needed expansion. Penetration and expansion. Accidentally, I drew two bullets together. I looked at what I had done. Maybe *that* was the answer. I sketched in a partition to separate the two bullets. The front bullet would be for quick expansion and the rear bullet would be for deep penetration. I wondered if such a bullet was made in any part of the world.

There was quite a bit of room in my old truck garage when all the vehicles were on the road. I had a metal lathe in the corner and a milling machine I had bought in San Francisco. Since I had the tools, I decided to try to rough out a bullet with a partition.

Roy Banta (my machinist) and I went to work. We made a hand press, then I went down to Los Angeles and bought a screw machine outfit. I also purchased some 5/16" copper rod and some lead. We ran that through and machined it down to .305", drilled both ends of it and pressed it into shape. In the meantime Fred Huntington, inventor of the RCBS Reloading Press and owner of the RCBS company, stopped by. He'd heard that I'd been working on a bullet, and Fred liked to take care of everybody. I had been using his older presses for years. He had some new presses he wanted me to buy. "Oh, Fred," I said, "I can't afford it." "Okay, I'm giving them to you," he said.

Fred drove a big old Packard touring car and carried all his gear in the back of that thing as he traveled around the country getting acquainted with everybody. In Oroville, California, Fred's father was in the laundry business, but Fred loved to hunt and started making all kinds of die and gun tools. Fred was a tremendous salesman. He would call on even the poorest reloader.

He had two sons, Fred Jr. and Buzzy. Fred built a big showroom and a store that Buzzy is running now. The place is huge with all types of game mounted on the walls and they stock a tremendous inventory of guns and equipment.

I made a number of trips to visit Fred later on. Fred was a great friend and became a tremendous booster of our products.

He would take over one of the motels in Oroville and a few of the restaurants and send out invitations to hundreds of people in the industry. They came from all over the world. He entertained them and put them up, and they toured his factory and store. Fred was wonderful at handling a crowd of people. I know he had at least a thousand people in Oroville. Since there weren't enough hotel rooms in town to handle everybody, he had people staying in friends' houses and with friends of friends. Buzzy is a chip off the old block in this regard.

Our copper rod came in 10– and 12–foot lengths. The rods were 5/16" (.3125) and a 30–caliber bullet was .308". We put the rod pieces into the lathe and machined the outside diameter (OD) down a little lower than .308", then made a special drill that would drill the hole, then run the reamer in there and make a tapered jacket out of it. Then we cut a few and ran a little pan full of those and put them in the lathe with the other end sticking out. We drilled that for the rear and

Nothing can compare to an October day with a rifle slung on your shoulder and elk bugling in the high timber.

the Partition "jackets" were ready. We made some very good–looking jackets. The hard part was forming the jackets into bullets. We didn't have any good way to get the lead in, so we'd melt the lead and let it drip in and harden.

Later we built some crude dies then tamped lead in each end and pressed them into bullets. We shot some and if you were real careful you could keep them on a pie plate. They were not match–grade bullets by any means, but I thought I might be able to hit a moose with one. 🦟

CHAPTER 13

One Shot, One Moose

We headed back to Canada in 1947 to hunt with Johnny Henderson in the same area we'd used before. This time, I brought along a shooting enthusiast named Clarence Purdy. He owned the Gopher Shooter Supply in Minnesota and put out a big catalog. At the time I think he was the biggest shot dealer that Winchester had. I got acquainted with him and we became good friends. I called him up, said I wanted to try some new bullets, and asked if he'd like to go along. "What do you mean new bullets?" he asked.

We met in Seattle and drove up to Canada. Along the way I explained everything I had been working on. He had hunted moose before but he hadn't had as much trouble knocking his moose down as I did because bullets shot through his 30–06 penetrated better than the faster 300.

There was no big problem getting close to the moose, because they weren't very wary. Once they started feeding on those willows, they were quite intent on them.

Clarence Purdy, using his 30–06, was the first hunter to take a moose with a Partition bullet. And he only needed one shot through the shoulder.

I came across a young bull, still plenty big, but I purposely took him because he was in some very deep jackpines and probably wasn't over 15 yards away. He just stood there and gave me plenty of time to shoot. I wanted to see what the bullet would do, punching through the brush to the moose on the other side. It probably didn't hit much brush going through there, but that new roughly–made Partition knocked him down right in his tracks.

We each filled our tags with bull moose with shoulder shots to put them down. The first thing I did was peel back the skin on each animal to see what had happened to the bullet. As crude as those first bullets were, they held up very well. We each had nice, expanded Partition bullets showing. And I couldn't help but feel a little proud of how well these bullets, *my* creations, had worked.

At the time, I had no thought of manufacturing the bullets myself, though I did want to see them commercially available. Magnum rifles were becoming more popular and it was obvious that better bullets would have to be made. *Someone* would have to make them.

When we hunted goats, I was out of Partitions and used some other bullets I'd brought along. I shot a goat and he took off and ran over the edge of a cliff. The wind had blown the snow way over the edge and he ran over that and jumped. I followed him over to see where he had gone and found myself out on that small ledge. As soon as I realized there was no ground under that snow, I backed up.

I couldn't imagine that anything could travel in that country much less live there. These goats walked the little tiny ledges and hopped from one to another like we would step from the street to the curb. To watch them jump from one rock to another small ledge is unbelievable. Their snow–white hair stands out brightly against the dark rock they so often are found on. It is very hard work to climb the rough rocky terrain to get within range. As long as you are below them, they don't seem to be afraid. But if you happen on them from above, they become very upset.

I loved hunting goats on our trips to British Columbia. In the fall, the males (billies) can be found in one area and the females (nannies) in a different one. I have never found them together in the fall. The females have the longest horns, but thinner than the males. The horn on a billy is heavier, though not quite as long.

The full hides make very fine throw rugs and the mounted heads are worth having on your wall. The first time I hunted goats, the weather happened to be very mild and clear. It was so clear that my friend and I had a terrible time judging the distance to the goat that I wanted. The dark rocks and the snow–white goats seemed rather close. So I took careful aim on the billy and squeezed the trigger. The bullet hit somewhat short of the animal. We guessed he was 150 yards away. In fact, the goat was over 300 yards from us.

Once we hired an Indian boy named Eddie to watch the horses. The boy had a little single–shot 22, but he didn't have any ammunition with him, so I gave him a box of ammo and I've regretted it ever since.

We left Eddie to watch the horses while we went after goats. Johnny made a special point of telling him to stay with the horses because they were tied on the side of a hill and could easily slip or break the lead rope or break off a branch. Also, there were a number of cougars in the area that might take advantage of an easy target like a horse.

Later in the day, Johnny and I were walking up a ridge. There was a lot of snow on the ground and we came across some blood. "Johnny, what do you think about this blood?" I asked, and Johnny said, "Cougar probably scratched deer good." We

A fine bull moose quartering toward the camera. "We each filled our tags with bull moose. The first thing I did was peel back the skin on each animal to see what had happened to the bullet. As crude as those first Partitions where, they held up very well."
~ John Nosler

went on and found some more blood in the tracks of another deer. Johnny guessed something was wrong. Then we saw Eddie on his horse. He had a goat tied on the back of it and he was out of bullets. He had shot all 50 of the 22 rimfires I'd given him, into every animal he'd come across. He shot every one. Of course, he finally got a goat cornered and got him down. Johnny got awful mad at him but the kid didn't care much.

We hunted that same area seven or eight times. Walt Remmy, Marion Mann, Donald O'Bleness, Guy Lewis, Don Low, Bob Van Vleet, and several others hunted with us up there. Van Vleet was with me when we saw the black cougar.

We were after goats and deer. The horns of the deer weren't as large as you find in the western United States, but their bodies were extremely large. There were very few moose in the area. It was some of the highest country in the area. Johnny picked up a young boy to watch the horses and stuff and we had a lot of fun with that kid. He didn't give a damn about the horses but wanted to be in on every other thing. We all got our goats but Bob Van Vleet. The guide said, "I'd like to move the party down by

Crossing the Fraser River in British Columbia

the lake because we'll have a better camp there." I knew right where the camp was so he said to me, "John, why don't you take Bob and do a little hunting on the way and you'll eventually get down there."

The guide said we were the first white people who had ever been in that area. He said to me, "John, I always take you someplace that white man has never been." We climbed a high ridge and were going down the other side. There were an awful lot of cougars up there. We smelled them when we went by the places where they had killed deer.

There was quite a lot of snow in some places so any movement caught our eye quickly. All of a sudden this black mountain lion came 90 miles an hour down the hill. It had caught our scent and spooked. When it hit a patch of snow and stuck its claws in, it just slid, dragging its claws to stop. It stood there, looking back toward where it had come from.

Bob had plenty of time to shoot. My gun was in my pack back at the lake. Bob took careful aim and squeezed the trigger. Click. He didn't have a cartridge in his

It takes a pack string of sturdy mountain horses to bring home the meat in British Columbia.

gun. Boy, that cougar flew back up that mountain faster than he had come down. That was the only black cougar I ever saw.

A little further on, we spotted a nice billy goat up on a rocky ledge. Bob, who had loaded his gun by now, shot it and we tried to go up to where it had fallen on a big flat rock. Every time we'd get on the rocky ledge leading up to it, the rock would teeter back and forth. That rock must have weighed several tons, but every time we stepped on it, it felt like it was going to give way and crash down the mountain. We were afraid, so we said, "Let's let Johnny come back and do this. He knows how to do this stuff." At least we'd tell him to bring a lasso and pull the goat off that deathtrap. So we went on back down and got the rest of the guys. Johnny did go up and gut that thing out without any problem.

Another time, Johnny, Marion Mann, and I went in there and ran into a lot of bear tracks. Johnny had terrible horses—big, fat lazy things. Every time we stopped, one of the horses would lie down. That was the biggest nuisance—you couldn't get him up unless you took the pack off him and by the time I'd done that three or four times a day, several days in a row, I was angry. I decided to buy that horse.

I kept after John, "How much would you take for that horse? I'd like to shoot him and put him out here for grizzly bait." I finally made a deal with John, giving him $35 for the horse. He'd never got $35 for any ten horses before. So I shot the horse and went out every day to wait for my grizzly to come, but black bears came in by the dozen and ate my horse all up. I finally shot a big black bear.

Johnny's wife Edith wanted the grease to use for cooking. Rendering that bear filled darn near half a galvanized washtub full of grease. She loved to cook with it. In fact, that's the only type of cooking oil she used. She'd make a cake but didn't have any fruit to put on it. Very seldom would we get pies unless we brought the fruit for her.

I always wanted a wolf hide to hang in the den, but I never had a chance to shoot a wolf. I had a million chances to buy hides, as every store had wolf hides for sale, but I wanted one that I had shot myself.

Johnny took me out to the Indian camps along the river, where the Indians hung game on poles for smoking. Small fires with a lot of smoke burned under them.

"I couldn't imagine that anything could travel in that country much less live there. These goats walked the little tiny ledges and hopped from one to another like we would step from the street to the curb. To watch them jump from one rock to another small ledge is unbelievable. Their snow–white hair stands out so bright against the dark rock they so often are found on. It is very hard work to climb the rough rocky terrain to get within range of them." – John Nosler

Walt Remmy with two fine Rocky Mountain billy goats from a hunt with John Nosler in British Columbia.

In every one of these places we would see totem poles the Indians had made. Why they made them and just left them I don't know, but it was beautiful work.

Traveling through, you'd meet a wagon coming down the road more often then you'd meet a car. Mostly it would be a bunch of Indian women. We'd always stop and ask them questions, but they wouldn't understand. They would giggle and we would giggle and smile, and eventually we'd go on our way.

I had a friend, Guy Lewis, an old railroader who lived in Ashland. His route ran down into Red Bluff and through Redding in the early days. I took him hunting when he was about 80 years old. He told us about running horse teams and freighters from Redding to Ashland before he started working for the railroad. He often jumped up and down off the trains when they were running. This did something to the bones in his legs that caused his legs to be amputated by the time I knew him. He had false legs from the knees down.

He loved to cuss and shoot and hunt. We took him with us when we could. He had hand levers adapted to the pedals of his Dodge pickup so he could drive. But he couldn't drive fast enough. O'Bleness had a GMC pickup that was faster than Lewis' Dodge. Every time they ran into each other around Ashland, O'Bleness would outrun him.

Guy got mad and he said, "John I want you to do something for my pickup because I don't want Don to pass me any more." So I rigged him up with dual manifolds and put two carburetors on it and it went pretty good. Nobody passed him again.

We had so much darn fun with him that we took him up to British Columbia with us. In fact, he drove his own Dodge pickup all the way there. He said he could ride a horse, but when we got him on one he just had to grit his teeth because it was so painful. His replacement legs were not adapted to riding in a saddle. But we finally got him out from Johnny's house a mile or two and spread out a canvas I had. He sat down with his 7 x 57 rifle. He really cussed us out when we came back to pick him up. He had shot a beautiful moose.

We were up there grizzly hunting in 1948 during a heck of a snowstorm. Johnny's dog Bounce would be running on the top of the snow and then all of a sudden he'd disappear. And you wouldn't see him and then he'd pop up 50–75 feet farther along. I'd never seen a dog do that before. But Bounce was well educated for the area.

We were headed home in my brand–new Dodge pickup when the exhaust pipe broke just in front of the muffler. Talk about noisy. It was loud and fumes were coming in the cab. We stopped at a little town with a store, farmhouse, and blacksmith. "Can you fix my muffler and weld it up today?" I asked the guy. He said, "I'll do it tomorrow." When we asked where we'd stay, he said, "I'll draw you a map. You go up to the ranch house and tell them I sent you up there."

The rancher had a large building with cars and old wagons and stuff in there. I saw a real old Chevrolet V–8, probably a 1915, or maybe 1916. Anyway, I fell in love with that thing. I knew it was rare. Chevy had built these experimentally to explore the luxury market, but sold them for only one year. I asked the guy what he'd take for it and he said $300. I said I'd send a truck to pick it up but I got so darn busy I forgot. I was down in Reno a few years ago and saw one of those cars at a museum. I asked the manager what it was worth. "Oh, probably a quarter million," he replied. So you win some and you lose some.

I continued to test my bullets on hunts in California and Oregon. I loved hunting in the Steens in Oregon. The Steens Mountains are nearly 10,000 feet above sea level and the big bucks stay up in the 9,000–foot range. You seldom see a doe and even less seldom a small buck. Every year I got better at it, and our camps became more comfortable. I also began to take more people with me.

One of my best hunting partners was Jack James. Jack is one of those great big good–looking men who stand straight and tall. When you talk to him you get the feeling he can accomplish anything he sets his mind to. He is also one of the best friends a man could ever want.

I met him before the war when we both were driving truck. He hauled cattle and later worked for one of the big contractors in southern Oregon. He joined the Army and worked as an engineer while stationed in Alaska and later on Okinawa.

After the war he started in construction again. He took on only large projects such as college additions, hospitals, and sawmills. Later in life, it was my privilege to see him honored as a "Builder of the Decade" by the State of Oregon.

Gravel Gerty was an old GI 4–wheel drive, owned by Jack James. An unfaithful old girl, the hunters could always depend on her to get deep into the backcountry and break down.

I owned five acres in Ashland not far from the college downtown. I became a councilman for the city and I got to know Dr. Stevenson, president of Southern Oregon State College. Dr. Stevenson and I were in the Lions Club together. The college needed land but didn't have a lot of money, so I donated 2½ acres of land which I didn't need anyway and they used part of that for their football field and a big gymnasium. Jack got the contract to put up the gymnasium within shouting distance of the old bullet plant. While they were laying out the project, he'd come up to the plant and bring coffee. We became very good friends.

Jack loved to hunt all types of game. And he could shoot right– or left–handed. Because he loved a challenge, he would often come over to my shop in the evening to help me solve a problem. Jack and I did a great deal of hunting together. He had an old Government–issued four–wheel–drive truck that had seen service before the

An all too–familiar scene. Gravel Gerty in Oregon's Trout Creek Mountains. Twice, Dick Alley was called and asked to locate a part. After a day or so, John's party would hear the sound of Dick's plane overhead and watch the needed parts parachute to the ground.

war. We called it Gravel Gerty. He fixed her and re–fixed her so we could take her in country where only four–wheelers could go.

We never relied on Gravel Gerty to get us out, just to get us in. She was an unfaithful old girl and her rear end was not in the best shape. We always had another pickup within walking distance, just in case she broke down. Once we had a very long walk out. We made it to a phone and called up our friend Dick Alley. We explained where he could find Gerty and told him what parts to pick up for the old girl. Then we walked back in. Dick flew over and dropped the parts down to us so we could put her back in working order and get her back on the road.

Gravel Gerty took us all over the Steens and Trout Creek Mountains and we made many of the roads over there that are still in use today.

There were very few people driving four–wheel–drive trucks in those days. Everybody drove their two–wheel–drive pickups, farm trucks, family cars, or whatever they had to hunting camp. To make up for the lack of traction, sometimes we chained as many as three rigs together. Chained them solid. You could push through a lot of mud with all six drive–tires turning.

One year I took Con Fury and Dr. Weller on a hunt. Con was stronger than hell. We were down in Kiger Canyon and we both had our bucks on the ground. I bent over to drag my deer around and gut him out, and my back snapped and went out. It hurt so bad I was practically paralyzed. When Con found me, he carried out his deer and mine.

Dr. Weller was a veterinarian and had never hunted or killed a deer in his life. After he shot his deer, he asked how to carry it out. "Just put it over your back, stick your hand up in the body cavity and carry it out," we told him. When he got to camp, he was covered with blood and guts, but he was smiling. He said, "I'm going to eat and enjoy every damn bit of it."

Once I was up on the Steens with Roy Banta (my machinist) and another friend of his from California. Each of us took a separate canyon. They were very far apart. "Just go down a little ways and you'll see deer in there," I told them. I got my deer first and was walking over to where Roy's canyon was because I had heard some shooting. As I came up to him, Roy said, "My deer is right over there." "Fine," I said, "let's go over and see the other guy and we'll pack up his deer and then yours and mine and head for home." When we got back to Roy's canyon, we couldn't find his deer though we hadn't been gone more than half an hour at most. "I know I shot it right here," he said. "I saw it," I said.

We went over to where the deer had been and saw some cougar tracks. We followed the tracks 400 yards to where the cougar had dragged the freshly killed deer and buried it in the brush. We dug the carcass out and Roy got his deer back.

My experimental bullets were working well. I was happy with how they performed on game and I knew other sportsmen would like them as well. I hoped I could find someone to make them and bring them to market. 🦌

CHAPTER 14

It Worked, So Now What?

I had heard of Sierra Bullets so I paid them a visit. They were operating out of an automotive dealership garage in Whittier, California. They had originally set up as a machine shop during World War II, working for Douglas Aircraft under the name of Harris Machinery. The end of the war meant the end of their contract so they began manufacturing bullets under the name of Sierra Bullets.

Clinton Harris owned the Oldsmobile dealership in Whittier. For a time he couldn't get any new Oldsmobiles, so he had space in the dealership garage. They set up their bullet–making operation in his building.

The men at Sierra were fine, honest, hard–working, nice–to–know people. Jim Spivey was the engineer, Frank Snow was an expert machinist, and Loren Harbor was the business expert. The bullets they were making were the cup–type and were most properly used for light hunting and target shooting. It was obvious to me that they were well organized and would be a fine company to work with. However, the line of presses they used in production of their bullets were not adaptable to manufacturing Partition–type bullets.

Spivey, Snow, and Harbor were keenly interested in the Partition bullet and wanted me to join them as a fifth partner. I was to put in some money and bring my bullet design along. I declined that offer because I didn't want to be a minor partner in a business.

While I was there they took me deep–sea fishing for albacore. The fish averaged about 18 inches in length. There were bunches of them; you'd get into a school and they would fight like crazy. We had some kind of a thing on for bait, not live, but some darn feathered jig. We used a short line and a strong pole and just pulled them

up over our heads onto the boat. That night, Loren Harbor and I worked until one o'clock in the morning, cleaning those darn fish.

Following this trip I went to Lewiston, Idaho, to see Vernon Speer who was making a line of bullets similar to Sierra's. He had one old Army press and was making Speer cup bullets with it. His machines could not be used for making Partition jackets.

I got to know Vern Speer's brother as well. He set up in Lewiston to make cartridge cases, eventually selling a bunch to Weatherby. The cartridge cases split badly, Weatherby sued him, and he had to shut down. But he did make some damn good primers. Well, they were good most of the time. He went to Germany and got a German engineer who knew a lot about primers, brought him over here and set up to make them.

Another good friend of mine was Dr. Cutter—a top physician and a very nice guy. He'd go elk hunting a lot. One day he said, "John, you're so proud of your damn bullets, would you fix me up with some for a 30–06?"

Speer had sent me three thousand of these primers as a goodwill gesture. When I was loading Cutter's elk hunting cartridges, I decided to use those primers. I'd used them once or twice and they seemed to work fine.

Bob Cutter went hunting and found his elk. Another guy from the other side of the canyon saw the same elk and fired at it. When they got to the animal, it had one bullet hole in it and they didn't know whose it was. So they shook hands and decided to divide it. They skinned it all out and Cutter found his Partition bullet. It was a sure thing that it was ours and Bob knew it, but he still gave the guy half the elk. Later he wanted to shoot his gun a little bit, just to see what it would do. He sat down on the ridge to shoot at some rocks across the canyon. He couldn't get the damn thing to fire one more time! None of the rest of the primers would fire. Bob was madder than hell at me. Those damn primers could have cost him (half) an elk.

Over time, I became well acquainted with Vern Speer and Joyce Hornady (Joyce Hornady used to work for Vernon Speer before he started up his own company). We'd meet at shows and hang around in Idaho at Johnson's Flying Service. Vernon Speer, Joyce Hornady, Jack James, and I were in Idaho once when a big storm came in. They were supposed to fly us into a place to hunt but nobody was flying in or out. We stayed there four or five days before we were able to leave and got well acquainted. Vernon Speer liked to come and fish the Deschutes River, and I welcomed him in our home. He had his own airplane (had been a World War II pilot), so every place he went he'd fly.

Building a bullet would be a very big undertaking. I had to make myself into an engineer. I began to study books on metallurgy and manufacturing. The library didn't have much to offer so I spent a lot of time in bookstores in bigger cities and sent away for books that other people told me about.

I decided to apply for a patent on my invention and learned that it would be easier if I flew directly to Washington, D.C., to get my patent in order. While I was there, I could go over and see the folks at Winchester.

I still didn't want to manufacture it because I already had a good business and didn't have the experience to bring a product like this to market. A good friend of mine who was an attorney was trying to get me a patent, but he didn't know anything about it. He associated himself with these patent attorneys that advertise in the back of magazines and I got thoroughly disgusted with what I was getting, so I said I was going to go back to work in D.C. and learn how to do it myself. I went to this group of patent attorneys that must have had twenty desks in a basement office. They were handling patents that were coming through the mail. They told me that they would take an initial fee, record it, then be through with it. This would cost about $100. People from all over the country would write in and contact these attorneys. Magazines had quite a few of these ads from similar firms. I talked to these fellows while working in D.C.

Next I went to the U.S. Patent Office. In those days, the Patent Office was similar to a large library. You tell them what you are interested in and then go to the desk and they give you a number. You go to that number and you find information on bullets and cartridges—reams and reams of information. You remove the items of interest from the shelves and take them to tables to study them, then leave them on the table when finished. You do not put anything back on the shelves.

I stayed in D.C. five days, searching and searching. Several men in suits from General Motors Company were using the table next to mine, studying automotive transmissions. After they left, I went over to see what was left lying on their table. It was the file on the Model T Ford's band system transmissions.

I found all the information I needed and applied for a patent myself, then climbed on the train and headed up to New Haven, Connecticut, to visit the Winchester plant. Like many other hunters, I thought Winchester was the absolute greatest. Winchester was very interested in the bullet samples I had with me. By golly, I thought, they'll take it over and make something out of it and I'll be happy and go home. They told me they would review it carefully.

I traveled home and waited for a letter from Winchester, telling me how they were going to manufacture it and how much they would pay me for my invention. I got a long letter. They thanked me for giving them the chance to review my idea, but they had decided not to spend the money it would take to explore its manufacture. It was just too darn strange and too different from the cup bullet. They had no machines to build it. They would have to put in different types of machines and that would be too costly and they didn't want to get into it.

I couldn't find anybody who was willing or able to build my bullet. I even looked in San Francisco and talked to a lot of shops in Los Angeles that had supplied products to the military during World War II. All were looking for something to do, but they didn't know how to do what was needed to make this bullet. For some time, it seemed I was the only one who thought a bullet like the Partition was needed.

I was fascinated with the whole idea. The more I dug into it, the more I thought it might be profitable, especially after watching the Sierra plant make their cup bullets for a week. They had a very nice organization and it looked like they were making a few bucks. So I thought, well, the bullet would sell, but one thing I didn't know was how much money it would cost before there were *any* bullets to sell.

I was a good mechanic and machinist, but I wasn't an engineer. My experience with engineers was that they didn't know anything about bullets—it takes a background with bullets to understand bullets. I don't know of anything made today, manufactured in volume, that requires any closer tolerance than a bullet does. When you look at a bullet like the very longest ones used in the 22–caliber, the 80 grains and up require a 7–inch twist, 1 revolution of the bullet in the barrel every 7 inches. By the time you get that bullet going over 3000 feet per second, your rotation has to be somewhere near 6000 revolutions per second. This is spinning fast, and 6000 revs per second is very difficult to understand. The centrifugal force is so powerful that some bullets explode in the air.

I finally decided to manufacture the bullet myself. I had been thinking about making it from tubing. I found a turret lathe (the size I thought might machine the tube and cut it off) in San Francisco. The copper tube suppliers would make tube with any copper–zinc content I specified and any wall thickness and size I wanted. I bought the minimum order of tubing and then went to work on a die system.

First I had to become a design engineer. A lot of what I needed to know could be found in books, so I bought or borrowed everything I could find about machine shop activities and engineering and studied every night after work.

Roy Banta had worked for Roy Weatherby, when Weatherby was first getting started. He was a big asset because he had tinkered around with making bullets for a guy who manufactured bullets in Los Angeles with a big hand press. Roy worked for me all the time I was in Ashland, and came to Bend with me and worked a number of years.

I could buy solid copper wire in the right dimensions and drill copper from each end which I did first just for an experiment. I bought an automatic lathe and set it up and got a lot of good experience with it. In fact, we tested for a full year before we sold anything. I finally came up with the idea of pressing a Partition in a tube. The copper people liked to use 90% copper and 10% zinc because it flowed better in a tube. This mix was a good choice for us.

First, we built a hand press, a great, big precision machine, powered by muscle. I hauled a little press in the back of my car up from San Francisco and used it to put the rear leads into the jacket. I needed a finish press, so I bought a 14–ton Diamond

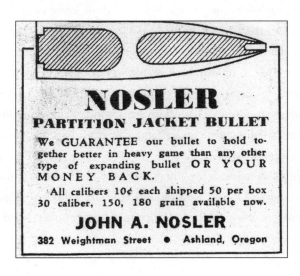

and sent it home in one of my trucks. The next day, I bought a 35–ton Niagara punch press and sent it home where we tooled it up to put the partition in the tubing.

After squeezing that metal together, we came up with a very nice jacket. It required no trimming at all and was ready for the lead cores. The die system I had designed worked well. We started out making that and I didn't want that solid metal 90–10 going through the rifling, so when the bullet was finished we ran it through a little automatic machine we had that would machine a groove down to bore size. We call it a relief. They were very good bullets.

The biggest problem that I had later was getting the dies to manufacture the tube with a uniform wall thickness all the way around, which was so crucial for accuracy. I bought a 40–ton press and we tooled it to form the Partition into the tubes. We had trouble making the dies. We broke a lot of them before we learned to make them strong enough to form the Partition in the tubes. By this time, I'd spent so damn much money doing it that I thought it might be a good idea to find a partner to share in the spending.

The next operation needed was to form the jackets with the front and rear lead cores in place into bullet shapes. I retooled the 14–ton press so it would tamp the lead core, then press the bullet and eject. We hand–fed this press also. I was now able to make a few Partition bullets. Every operation was slow, so very few bullets were made in a day's work.

But I finally had bullets in production. So I began sending them out to see what the gun writers thought of them. Herb Klein, a wealthy hunter from Texas, carried our bullets to Africa. In his book, *Lucky Bwana,* he called them "the world's deadliest bullet."

As our bullets gained fame around the world, I began to make friends with prominent gun writers, and manufacturers in the industry. I sent some bullets to Elmer Keith. He turned out to be a very good booster, promoting our bullet in magazine articles and books.

Elmer Keith was a proponent of the big calibers and became a good friend of mine. We wrote letters back and forth for years. He had no use for the 270–class rifles except for shooting very small game. I could understand his thinking because of my experiences hunting moose with the 300 Winchester Magnum. During Elmer's early years, a bullet that could penetrate and expand was not available, except for those in low–velocity rifles like the 30–40 Krag and the 300 Savage. You couldn't even get a good bullet for the 30–06. So Elmer found rifles like the 300 Win Mag to be poor on big game. The large–caliber, heavy bullets, fired at much slower velocities, penetrated and left a big hole. He was a good shot and made a number of long shots with his big rifles. He was very much right in choosing the big bores. In his time, his pick of hunting guns was right on.

I corresponded with Elmer for many years. He was keenly interested in the Partition bullet. He was a partner in O'Neil, Keith and Hopkins (OKH); O'Neil was a gunsmith and hunter, and Hopkins was a wealthy attorney who loved to hunt in Africa. OKH developed souped–up cartridges based on standard cartridges. The 426 OKH was based on the Westley Richards 425 and the 285 OKH Wildcat was developed for sheep hunting and was made by necking the 30–06 case down to 7mm. To build the 333 OKH, they necked up a 30–06 case to hold the 333 bullets that were used by the 333 Jeffrey. The 333 Belted used a short magnum case for the same bullet. Another of their projects was based on the 470. They called it the 475 OKH. They developed a primer tube that extended the primer to the fore part of the cartridge and ignited the forward part of the powder first. I later got several of these and played with them, and thought their design had a certain amount of merit.

Keith took their primer tube to the government during WWII and the government did quite a bit of research with the 50–caliber machine guns used in airplanes. It did give them a little more velocity, which they were keenly interested in, but I think the cost was too prohibitive to get into in wartime. However, Elmer got quite a bit of recognition for his work with OKH.

Once when I was taking the family up into Canada, I phoned Elmer ahead of time and we stopped in Salmon, Idaho, to visit with him. Elmer picked us up and we had dinner up there at his house, and spent a night and the next day there. Salmon had a real frontier town atmosphere. The Indian reservation was close by and there was a large group of Indians camped out in wigwams.

Elmer had a fascination for revolvers. "Let me show you my collection," he said, and pulled out a 3–foot–high by 5–foot–long trunk, an old round–lid type of thing held together with straps. He opened it up and it was absolutely full of single–action Colts.

I looked them all over and fooled around with them and he said, "Well, go ahead and take one of them." I passed because I didn't want to take one up into Canada, but asked him to reserve one for my next visit. Elmer and I became pretty good friends after that. We got together on different occasions and I wrote him letters, asked his opinion on new ideas and some old ideas, and sent him a lot of bullets. He gave me his comments, which I valued.

I'm not sure he really knew what he was running into, but Elmer did have some experience on high–velocity rifles with heavy game. I'm quite sure that he had the same problem with bullet disintegration on impact that I had experienced. So he kept looking back at the big bore, slower–velocity type that would penetrate anything. He wasn't wrong, but he was recommending a large caliber. You could shoot it as fast as you could stand up your shoulder to it, and still you wouldn't be shooting the bullet very fast. His theory was good.

I sent some 220–grain Partition bullets in very strong jackets to Elmer with the words, "You don't believe that a 30–caliber bullet will kill a buffalo? Take some of these and next time you feel like shooting a buffalo (American Bison, which he shot quite often) try one of these." He said you had to use at least a 375 on a buffalo and preferably a bigger gun with a bigger bullet. So he would never do it or if he did he never told me about it. But I doubt if he would have told me anyway.

He had a big house on a hill with a large front porch clear across the front of the house with rocking chairs out there. You could stand and look out on the town, and watch the Indian gatherings from his porch. Inside, it was a simple, plain house, really clean; his wife was a good housekeeper. They had a wood stove and an electric cook stove too. He had a few game heads on the wall and a lot of skins hanging around. He wasn't too much for mounting heads. Probably no one around close to do it anyway. He drove a big Buick car probably 5 years old and I had a brand–spanking–new Buick Roadmaster sedan. Boy, he fell in love with that car of mine and he was trying his darndest to make a deal with me—to do anything. He said, "I'll write you a whole bunch of good articles." But I said, "No, Elmer, that isn't going to work." I *think* he was kidding. We were good friends up to his death.

I had a great deal of respect for Warren Page. I didn't get to know him real well, but I had met him on two or three occasions at industry functions. He was a 7 mm fan, had a Magnum not too much different from the 7 mm Remington, maybe a little bigger case, and he thought that was the greatest thing. I guess it was. He loved the Partition bullet and said he shot absolutely nothing else. I believed him because I think he definitely needed Partition bullets. A good hunter, a very good writer, and an awfully nice guy.

I really liked Jack O'Connor. I was up at Jack's place a few times in Lewiston, Idaho. I often went there to visit with Vernon Speer. We had no secrets between us. We'd talk over our problems and he'd give me ideas, and maybe I gave him some. But he was a good guy to know. Being up there I would go visit Jack and his wife. Jack was very friendly, a little tough to get acquainted with right off the bat, but after you did, he was very interesting. Of course, he loved that 270. He used Speer's facilities so much, their shooting tube and all, and got free access to their chronograph that he had to promote them quite a bit. And I don't blame him at all, but I know he used the Partition a lot too and found out that it did things the other bullets couldn't.

Jack thought that he'd like to shoot sage hens. So he came down and shot a few sage hens and visited with us. We wined and dined him, and enjoyed our time together.

Jack O'Connor later wrote in his book, *The Art of Hunting Big Game*, "If I am in grizzly country I take with me a few cartridges loaded with the 150–grain Nosler bullet at around 2950, and either (rifle) will put this heavier bullet to the same point of impact as the lighter ones to 200 yards. There are other combinations just as good for sheep, no doubt, but I can't think of a better one."

Finally I was doing what I had set out to do and we were hard–pressed to keep up with the demand. We had proved the Partition was needed. I resolved to go all out to manufacture and sell Partition bullets.

The next thing to do was to tool every operation up with the best possible machines and die systems. All operations had to run automatically. I would also need a larger building because I was outgrowing my old truck repair shop. I began to look around.

Louise was keeping the books and keeping me in line. All I was doing was spending the money I had made in the trucking business. Every time I went anywhere, I stopped at libraries and bookstores and filled my car up with books on engineering. I was in San Francisco a lot with my business, and I bought out the bookstores on engineering stuff and found out all I could. It was the way to go, there's no doubt about it. I had to teach myself engineering and gather as much of the right equipment as I could. No one else was going to do it for me.

I was up in Portland looking at an automatic screw machine and I went to a fellow's house there in the city and he had some screw machines for sale. I was parked out in front of his place talking to him and instead of talking about the

Inside Nosler's first bullet plant in Ashland, Oregon.

93

machine he wanted to tell me about his new method of hunting elk. Of course, I had to hear all about that.

He said one of his buddies had an airplane and would fly around until he spotted a herd of elk. Then he waggled the wings so the hunters on the ground would know where the elk were. The hunters would go over there as fast as they could. Killing those elk was no problem at all. Just as he said that, a car pulled up behind us and a policeman came over and asked, "Are you Mr. Kline?" The guy said he was and the policeman said, "You are under arrest." Well, that put him out of the airplane business. I bought the screw machine from him while the state police put the screws to him.

I bought one machine after another to get closer to making a few Partition bullets. At first I would sketch up a simple machine that would do some part of the process just so I could have bullets to test. Then I would figure out another operation to make it faster. I spent many a day on the drawing board after an idea came to me about what was needed.

Making the Partition from tubing required many operations. We started with an automatic lathe made by Brown and Sharpe. The 12–foot copper tube came in boxes. We'd put another tube in the machine and the thing would start working right away. They weren't real fast but they were a lot more than a man could do on a hand–operated press. I ended up with six screw machines. They chopped up the copper really fast.

Each machine had to be tooled and fitted to do the job required. Then we needed an operator and an operator's helper. From there, the parts were washed, acid–dipped, rinsed, dried, then a thin coat of a special wax was applied which then dried while rotating in a basket.

The jackets were hopper–fed into a large press that had a top and a bottom punch in a floating die that formed a partition in the tube. From there, the jackets went to a smaller press that had an operator insert the rear lead core. The press would tamp the core in and then crimp the jacket over the lead core.

We made the lead cores in a press I designed for feeding lead wire. The wire was pulled into the machine by a cam arrangement in precise amounts (lengths). Each piece was sheared off and placed into a die, followed by a punch, which pressed it into a precise shape to fit the jacket.

The finish press that forms the jacket into a complete bullet has several stations. The first drops the lead core into the jacket. The next tamps the core into the jacket. Subsequent stations press the jacket to the first pointing die, then press it again to fully form the bullet. Additional operations can also be done such as feeding in a plastic tip or rolling a cannelure (a serrated groove that serves as a notch for crimping the case neck into the bullet).

All this time, Louise was working with me in the shop as well as in the office, answering letters and filling orders. I got all the machines working to make a few bullets, not on a big scale but we were making some. I had it all mechanized pretty well but some of the machines had to be hand–fed. Ron was attending Junior High and he'd come home after school to run the Partition hand press. He was very dexterous and was a great help when he wasn't doing homework.

Ron would pick up a jacket, put the lead in, and set it on a pin. It would get tamped, sized, and ejected and then those jackets with the rear leads would go through the finish press. With no hopper or front lead mechanism yet, we made the leads on a separate machine as a temporary measure.

Louise would pick up the front lead and set it in the die while the press was running. You had to be pretty dexterous to do that and the press would tamp that in good and tight, then move it over and press the bullet, then move it over and eject it . . . and get ready for another one. I needed a larger building and many more machines if I was ever going to get this thing to work.

After the bullet business started to look like it was going somewhere, I wanted to make bullet displays. We put together 1500 of them. We would sell some of them and give others to gun stores to display the Partition bullets. I would include one in cross–section and one fired bullet to give an example of the mushroom.

To obtain the mushroomed bullets, I would fire them into water. I had done this many times before to get fired samples to examine. The big problem was what to fire 1500 bullets into that would be strong enough to hold water through 1500 rounds. I hoped to use 55–gallon (former) oil drums filled to the top with water.

Jack James had a small ranch nearby with a barn and a loft just the right height for our little project. We rounded up ten old oil drums. Jack would fire the 300 Winchester Magnum. The first few shots proved the oil drums weren't the right choice. The concussion split them after two or three shots.

Jack had a heavy steel bucket he used to pour concrete. It held about 100 gallons of water. So we used it for the rest of the project. Firing 1500 shots is more work than one might expect. Especially from a 300 Win Mag. After about ten rounds, the barrel would heat up too hot to hold. So we changed jobs. I would come down the ladder with the very hot gun barrel and cool it with water. Then Jack would go up and fire, while I would de–prime and prime and dip the cases in the powder, gauge the load by eyeball, seat the bullets, and throw the loaded cartridges up to Jack to fire.

Everything was wet. Each shot would splash water all over. I would do this differently today, but experience is a good teacher. A few of those old bullet displays are still around and I'm told some of them bring very high prices these days.

I sold the trucking company piece by piece. I had several trucks and sold one truck and a grocery hauler to one of the fellows who worked for me. He bought the oldest truck I had, the 1940 Peterbilt, and made a good living from it. Then I sold one to a logger who was well versed in logging trucks.

He bought the newest one, a 1952 Peterbilt cabover with beautiful aluminum boxes and a utility trailer. He put a couple of relatives to work on it but they could never master backing up a full truck and trailer. They just let the tongue go as far as it could and then pushed the trailer on back and it would jackknife and skid. And right in the middle of San Francisco while they were going down one of those hills, the fifth wheel busted loose and pulled out from under the trailer, and the nose went down flat on the road. So one day he came back to me and told me his boys just couldn't handle the truck and trailer and asked what I thought. I said "Well, I'll try and sell it for you but I'm not going to take it and give you your money back."

Another friend of mine, an Italian named Tony Caruso, was hauling produce in the Portland area. He said he wanted to buy a truck van and full trailer like the one I had. So he bought the van and trailer from the logger who bought a trailer that his boys could handle and everyone was happy.

I went fishing when I needed a break from trucks and shooting and bullets. I fished a lot, quite a bit in Ashland and in Bend. We loved Diamond Lake in the Cascades. There was a period at Diamond Lake when I'd get up there an hour before dark, get the boat in the water, and pretty soon just as the sun went down the fish would start biting and we'd get a few nice trout before it turned dark.

Whenever I spent much time on the water, I got to thinking about business again, especially the business of shooting. That quiet time gave me the opportunity to think. I needed capital to finance our growth. I needed a partner.

CHAPTER 15

Bull's-eyes, Blacktails and a
Partner in the Bullet Business

Business partnerships happen because you need additional capital. Our bullet business was no exception. By 1954, Louise and I had poured our life savings and the proceeds of the trucking company into the bullet business and we needed help.

Starting a new business is like nursing a sick child. You don't scrimp and you don't hold back. The whole family turns their focus onto getting the child well. We could see this child had a bright future if we could just get it through its formative years.

My old friend and hunting companion, Don O'Bleness, had sold his automobile dealership and was looking for something else to do in his retirement. He was looking to invest his money in the hopes of getting a return on it in a few years. He and his wife joined Louise and me in taking our business to the next level. As partners, we worked together well. His wife and Louise worked with us in the shop building bullets as well as filling orders, answering letters, and sweating over the books.

Don became my partner in 1954, buying in at a 50 percent ownership level. We kept adding machines as we could afford them. I knew that before any real money was made, the bullet jacket would have to be extruded. Nobody extruded anything in the United States until after World War II. The people I asked said that too much labor was involved. They said it was too expensive, but I needed to do something different to reduce the waste of materials.

A 20% scrap loss in your raw material is hard to swallow. I was dead set on learning extrusion because I could see that was the only way we could cut our scrap loss and bring the bullets to the public at a reasonable price. In the 1950s, nobody was working with extrusion except General Motors and Ford Motor Company.

The extruding material would be wire instead of tubing. The wire would be sheared off instead of machined. Hardly any scrap loss and the process would be much cheaper.

But before I could get into extrusion, I had to have a bigger building. The college wanted to buy my five acres. I had given Southern Oregon College two–and–a–half acres of my land to put up their gymnasium and make room for their football field.

They wanted the rest of it whenever I was going to get rid of it. In fact, they insisted that I couldn't sell it to anybody but them. I was on the city council in Ashland at that time and the city was abandoning a warehouse.

Eventually, we moved into the abandoned warehouse but I could see that soon we would outgrow that building as well. As our company grew, so did our visibility in Ashland. The city fathers were not all that friendly toward the shooting sports. I began to wonder if we should find another place to do business.

A box of the early, lathe–turned 30–caliber Partitions built in Ashland, Oregon.

It was about this time that I met two people who became very important in my life in later years. First I met Jack Slack, of Leupold and Stevens, at a gun show. Leupold and Stevens were marketing their products all over the country. Jack came to see me in Ashland many times. He was very interested in what I was doing and I was very interested in the scope business. Marcus Leupold, the head of Leupold and Stevens, also came often. His wife was a fan of the Shakespearean Festival in Ashland. Marcus brought her down to attend the plays and they would stay a week or so. He didn't like the shows, so he'd visit where I was working to talk and exchange ideas, and we'd have lunch together.

I was still shooting in competitions. Little Bob wanted to come with me so I made him a short little 22 rimfire with a scope and sling. He would fire all evening on his target while the rest of us were shooting the four-position shoot. Everyone marveled at how a five-year-old could take it all so seriously. He went hunting with me every chance he could from then on. I took him on many blacktail hunts in Ashland.

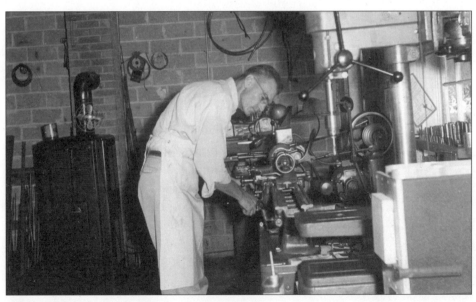

John working on lathe in Ashland, Oregon plant.

I wanted to get a saddle horse for myself. There were quite a few wild horses in eastern Oregon. I bought one from a fellow in Klamath Falls who had caught several. He sold me a nice little mare that was about half broke. Ron and his mother named her Gypsy. We had a lot of fun with her.

When Bob got a little older, he decided he wanted a horse too. I bought an old horse from a guy in the neighborhood and Bob named her Stinky. He never had a saddle for her, but he did have a bridle. She was so gentle she didn't even need a bridle. That horse knew more about kids than the kids knew about themselves.

One fall morning Bob, Guy Lewis, and I went blacktail hunting in some country with big rolling hills and a few oak trees. There was a lot of rimrock in that area and some poison oak. We hiked up to the rim; I would lift Bob up first and then climb up after him. Bob was growing tired and asked me to take him back to the truck where Guy was waiting for us. I took Bob back to the truck and went on hunting. I came up to a large rimrock and was climbing up when a large timber rattler struck at me and jumped into the air. It shook me up so much I didn't shoot it after it landed some distance from me on the rimrock. If Bob had still been with me, I would have lifted him up there and the snake would have hit him instead.

When Bob was about eight years old, I gave him a brand–new little deer rifle chambered for the 250–3000 Savage. He and I and two other guys were hunting

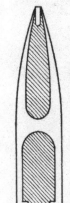
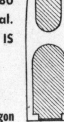

over in the Green Springs area in southern Oregon. We saw quite a few blacktail deer but didn't shoot any. Bob was tagging along. While we were moving from one spot to another in the car, he spotted one. He said, "Dad, there's a deer right in there." He had spotted it before me, but it had no antlers. We went on and parked our car in an old rock quarry and climbed up to the top.

On our way back to the truck we hit the edge of that quarry again. "Bob," I said, "do you think you could make it down the slope?" He thought he could. And I said, "If we don't, we'll have to walk about a mile–and–a–half to get around to the pickup." Bob said, "Let's slide down."

We started down and kicked up a nest of yellow jackets on the side of the hill, and they just boiled out of there by the hundreds and lit on little Bob. I never even knew they were there until I saw Bob slapping himself, but we were sliding fast and I was trying to stop and catch him. I finally did and saw what was happening. Even though he was being stung so bad, he wouldn't drop his new gun. We stepped on down and he was absolutely covered with yellowjackets just stinging the hell out of him. I yanked his shirt off and stripped him down. They were all over him.

I was afraid little Bob wasn't going to make it, he'd been stung so many times. I got him home, called Doc Haines and told him what had happened. He came out and looked Bob over and said, "Let's get him in the bathtub." We poured in a whole bunch of baking soda and let him soak in the tub while the baking soda took some of the burn out of stings.

Doc Haines loved to hunt. His theory was to bark like a dog. I'd seen other guys do that too. He said a lot of the deer that you would pass would stay bedded down. A hunter would never get to see them and I know that's a fact. But if you bark like a dog they'll get up and run ahead of you, and you eventually see them. It sure sounded funny listening to him do that.

We still had deer tags so we headed over to my old hunting area in the Steens in eastern Oregon. After driving all night, we slept in the pickup then had breakfast in Frenchglen and drove up to my old camp. Bob and I started down the ridge and I shot a four–point about 150 yards away. I put Bob on a rock and told him to wait there for me while I went down and took care of my deer. It wasn't long before I heard his rifle. He had just bagged his first deer with a Nosler bullet.

I was proud of my little boy. As we headed back for Ashland and he dozed in the cab of the truck, I couldn't help but think that a lot of hunters would someday take their first deer with Nosler bullets, if we could continue to bring them to the market. But once again events beyond my control were taking shape across the globe.

CHAPTER 16

Bumpy Going in Canada and Crowfoot

Copper and lead became hard to find as the Korean War heated up. Finally I couldn't buy it at all. The military was using up all the copper, buying bullets to shoot Communists in Korea. Since I couldn't make bullets I decided to take some time off. I would spend it in Canada, of course. I wanted to explore building a ranch in British Columbia.

Louise and I and the boys drove up to look at the country. I wanted my family to see what I had seen, but I couldn't show them much from the window of the Roadmaster. We drove into Vancouver and I inquired of the government how much they would sell the land for and what the requirements were. I thought that if I bought the land I'd get the timber. That was a mistake. The Canadian government owned all the mineral and timber rights.

You were allowed to use all that you wanted for your personal use but you couldn't sell it. I was hoping to acquire a bunch of that timber and put up a sawmill and sell the wood back in the States. I figured I could come up with a hell of a nice ranch in there, though I might have to take a Caterpillar in there to make the roads better. But it took the wind out of my sails when I found out I couldn't take advantage of the timber, so we decided to just vacation up there. We went way up the Alaska Highway. I wanted to drive all the way into Alaska, but we met up with a family in a Volkswagen van at a little store. Most of the windows had been busted out of the thing. It looked as if it had rolled over about 16 times. Louise started talking to the lady who told us what had happened, saying that she was so glad to get out of that country. She said they'd rolled the thing on the terrible roads they had come in on. Nobody got hurt but they had papers and cardboard for windows. So Louise was all for turning around.

Heading south, we stopped in Dawson Creek and heard they were opening up a new highway. We decided we'd stay over a day or so and try it out. The Governor General of Canada was coming over and a bunch of officials were going to have a caravan to open up the new road. I don't know how many times they had to pull us through a mud bog with the Cat on the new highway. We found out that the Governor's committee only went down about 15 miles and then they turned around and came back. So we were hooked on the thing and had to go all the way. My headlights were always covered with mud. I would get out to clean them and in a few miles I couldn't see where I was going.

We finally came to a small place between Prince George and Quesnel and found a roadhouse. A party was going full blast but none of us felt like celebrating anything. All I could think about was getting some sleep. A Royal Canadian Mounted Policeman asked, "Are you people thinking about staying here? I'd advise you not to." We finally got one bed for all of us. Louise rolled back the sheet and saw an earring in the bed. She wouldn't sleep there but I didn't care, I was so damn tired. I had driven all night long and all day before we arrived.

On our way back to the United States, we ate lunch at a hotel in Edmonton. Bob was drinking a Coke, but Ron wanted a malted milk. We ordered one and the girl brought it. Ron took a sip and said, "Dad, this doesn't taste good." And I said, "You wanted it, now drink it and shut up." So he went to his mother and said, "This tastes terrible." Louise took a little taste of it and said, "John, it *is* terrible." We called the waitress over. It turned out that they had a soap dispenser right next to the malt dispenser and had given it a shot of soap instead of malt.

We drove back through Banff National Park and Yellowstone. In those days almost everyone fed the bears right out of the car. The bears were so damn friendly that they wanted to get into our car. When I wasn't paying attention, Ron lured a bear through the window and into the back seat with him and Bob. Imagine my surprise when I looked in the rear view mirror and saw a black bear looking back at me.

Even if I couldn't make bullets for awhile I could still shoot them. I used the time off to learn more about engineering and spend time with friends—target shooting, hunting, and fishing.

Dick Alley operated a sawmill in nearby Medford and sold lumber up and down the coast. Dick was a good friend. He was a test pilot in WWII and loved to fly. His dad started a lumber business in Medford, and bought up a whole bunch of timber. They built a big sawmill there and a planing mill. They developed a sales organization in Los Angeles in a big building at the old airport and filled that with their salesmen. So Dick got the mill from his dad, and in those days you couldn't do anything wrong in the lumber business. Dick and his son Tom were good sportsmen and good friends. We hunted together a lot with Jack James.

Once, Francis Cheney, Jack James, Dick Alley and I headed up to Northeast Oregon to hunt elk. A friend of ours let us use his hunting cabin. Dick brought along one of his shop foremen, a fellow named Ed.

Dick Alley and John Nosler pause for an afternoon break during a moose hunt in British Columbia. Over the years, John took close to 30 moose in BC and Alaska.

At the end of the first day we gathered back at the cabin. Everyone was bone-tired from hunting all day. We put our guns away and relaxed with a few drinks. No one bothered to make dinner, we just ate what was easy to grab. Ed had a few more drinks than the rest of us. He grabbed a knife and cut a chunk of smoked elk meat and tried to wash it down with a swallow of beer. The chunk of meat lodged in his throat. He fell off his chair with both of his hands clamped around his throat. He couldn't get a breath and you could see the fear in his eyes. He pounded on the ground and tried to get our attention. No one had ever heard of the Heimlich Maneuver, but Jack James had heard that you could cut open a man's windpipe and remove the blockage that way. We knew he had to hurry or Ed was going to die right there in front of us.

Jack was still wearing his six-inch hunting knife. He whipped it out and bent down over poor Ed and put the point of the blade against his throat. I thought Ed's eyes were going to pop out of his head. "Where do I cut? Which way should I cut?" Jack asked, "sideways, or up and down?"

Finally, Jack decided to cut it sideways, and that was more than Ed could take, somehow he got a breath and the meat came out and he lay on the floor gasping, keeping Jack at arm's length.

We also hunted in Idaho in the high mountains along the Salmon River. Once we went in by air with Johnson's Flying Service to a little strip called Crowfoot. The pilot had to fly between two very high cliffs, before making a very sharp turn to land. The landing strip was on an uphill slope. It took two trips to get Jack James, Dick, and I in there.

The guides' quarters were uphill at the end of a Jeep road into the mountains. We hunted on foot but had horses to help us pack out game. From the lodge to the river we went by Jeep. They used a motor boat to take us across the river. It was a mile hike uphill to where we hunted. We left before daylight and it was still early when we got to the hunting area. The elk were bugling, so I planned to try luring one to me. I was able to bugle with my voice pretty well, so I set up in a place where I could see for some distance and I began to call.

A bull came to my call, but he wasn't as big as I was looking for so I didn't shoot. I also wasn't too excited about loading up the airplane with all that meat. I spent the rest of the day calling but had no luck. It was a beautiful place to sit and look at the scenery. At the end of the day I found Dick and we hunted down to the river together.

None of us made a kill that day because we were worried about getting our game back out safely. The weather was getting bad. We stood out on the landing strip the next morning, wondering whether we would be able to fly out. Just then, the plane came in. Dick and Jack went out and I stayed with the bags, ready for the next trip. We seldom ended hunts without some game to take home, but this place was too risky to chance getting any meat out.

I was sitting on my bedroll watching the storm roll in, when the plane came back for me. As I was loading my gear, I heard the pilot's orders coming over the radio. "Don't go into Crowfoot. Repeat. Do *not* fly into Crowfoot." The pilot said, "Jump in. They don't know I'm already here."

Off we went. It was very bumpy going out but the pilots that fly into that country are very good. We seemed to be no more than a couple of feet away from the cliff as we flew out. I was very happy to be home after that trip.

Finally, we were able to buy copper and lead again. We had been receiving letters from hunters, asking for more bullets. I was excited to get started again.

"When you know you're close to elk, slow down and keep the wind in your face. Still–hunting in the brush can be a very effective way to get close to the herd."
– John Nosler.

CHAPTER 17

The Industrial Committee

William Dawkins was a freelance writer from Ashland. Along toward the end of 1955, he interviewed me for a story he hoped to sell to *The Oregonian*, Oregon's largest daily newspaper. On February 5, 1956, Don O'Bleness and I were pictured on the front page of the Sunday edition of the Oregonian's *Northwest Magazine*. I was seated at a shooting bench and Don was holding a scoped, bolt–action rifle. The article was called "Their Bullets Are the Deadliest."

In Bend, Oregon, the Industrial Committee was looking for small businesses to help fill the void of the fading lumber industry. They read the article in *The Oregonian* and called me on the telephone to arrange a meeting. In less than a week, their representatives were standing in our office. They thought our little growing business was just what Central Oregon needed. I loved the hunting east of the Cascades, so I wasn't very hard to convince.

Bend was a lot different then. It hadn't yet grown up into the bustling city it is today. The only good paying jobs in town were at the mill or with the government. The forward–thinkers in town were desperate to bring in more employment, to give Bend a future beyond timber.

The Industrial Committee asked Pat Metke to negotiate our move. So Pat called and asked if I would come over and bring my two boys along. We drove over and met with Owen Panner, Bob Chandler, and Chuck Cleveland and they showed us all the available land.

We had lunch at the Pine Tavern downtown. A one–way alley ran from the restaurant out toward the old Post Office two blocks away. Ron and I noticed that the locals liked to use the alley as a shortcut, going either way. So when it was time to head home to Ashland, Ron drove into the alley, headed against the Do Not Enter sign, just like a local.

As Ron pulled out onto Franklin Avenue, I saw a policeman pull in behind us. Then the flashing lights came on. Apparently, the officer wasn't on the Industrial Committee. I told him that we'd just gotten there and didn't know how the streets worked. He said it didn't make any difference, and we had to go to the police station. We went to the station and they fined Ron for driving the wrong way on a one–way street. I told them, "I'm not moving to this damn town. I'm not moving over here." It wasn't fair that the locals could drive like that but not us out–of–towners. I went home and healed up and got over it.

The bullet plant on Parrell Road in Bend, Oregon. Circa 1960.

John Nosler at the plant. "Merchants from all over town donated time, money, and materials to help us make the move to the new plant. The citizens of Bend were very good to us and I've never regretted moving to central Oregon." – John Nosler

I had my eye on some property on Parrell Road. The guy who owned it offered to donate two acres. They had to run water over to Parrell, because there was no city water there yet. They ran a one–inch line, and by the time the pipe bore the water all the way there, there wasn't enough pressure, so the City put in a cistern for us. The ditch water ran along the property line in back so I had the choice of using ditch water also. The only problem with the ditch water was that it had a little foreign substance in it that we found, when rinsing the bullet jackets, caused our dies to wear too fast. We went back to using city water.

We drove up to Bend from Ashland on weekends, looking for a place to live. By this time Ron was 22 and Bob was 12 years old. I had some business at U.S. Bank

Inside the Nosler bullet plant as it looked in the 1960s.

so Louise and the kids waited outside in our little Ford station wagon. The car was parked on Minnesota Avenue, right next to the original location of the landmark Masterson–St. Clair Hardware store. Clippety–clop, clippety–clop. Along came an Indian woman mounted on a pony, towing a travois with a child behind her. She rode down the street and out of sight. All was quiet in the car as Louise and the kids tried to reconcile what they had seen in the street of our new hometown. Finally Louise whispered, "Where in God's name has your father brought us?"

A fellow named Bernie Price with Consolidated Freightways volunteered to bring two truck–and–trailer rigs over to haul all of my equipment for free to help the city of Bend. All I had to do was move my personal belongings.

Merchants from all over town donated time, money, and materials to help us make the move. The citizens of Bend were very good to us and I've never regretted moving to Central Oregon.

Three of our Ashland employees moved with us. Roy Banta was my machinist at the time. A young engineer named Dee Hillberry was helping me then. He was going to school at Oregon State University and would come over to work for me when school was out.

Ron Nosler in the 1950s.

Bob Nosler and Don O'Bleness with a mule deer taken in eastern Oregon.

114

Dee was a shooter too. He and I went hunting on the east side of the Steens once. We took some other friends and little Bob. Dee, Bob, and I went clear to the top on the other side, the steepest side. Dee saw a nice buck and shot it and we were sitting there tired and wondering how long it was going to take us to get down. Another buck popped up and I shot him. I got his antlers and backstraps and hindquarters on my backpack and Dee did the same. At the time I shot there were three or four does within about 150 yards or so. We saw them jump off a huge rimrock way over and down. They must have dropped 50 feet on purpose. Why they did that I don't know, but they did it even though they didn't have to.

We started on down and I damn near lost everything including myself going down that steep slope. The ground was white and powdery, very slippery. I was hanging onto a tree with the full pack on my back, and suddenly the whole land slipped out from under me and I was left hanging with my feet dangling hundreds of feet above anything.

I had to get rid of that pack 'cause I was afraid the damn tree might go down. I twisted out of the pack and said goodbye to it. The last I saw of my deer was its antlers way up in the air. I managed to climb around that tree and get up on solid ground, and we made it down in fine shape.

Not long after we moved, Ron joined the Air Force. He was stationed in Newfoundland for most of his enlistment. Afterwards, he returned to Oregon and attended Southern Oregon State College in Ashland where he majored in English. We missed him at the plant in those years, and were happy when he came home to visit.

At the plant, we were feeling the strain of an old friendship grown too familiar by way of a business. All partnerships, good and bad, eventually come to an end. Don O'Bleness had seen enough of the bullet business by 1958 and he wanted out. I began to look for a new partner.

CHAPTER 18

A Bullet and a Grizz

I knew I was going to need another partner because I didn't want to spend all the money I had left. When I talked to my accountant, he told me about a friend of his, a wealthy ex–lumberman named Ray Wade, who was familiar with our bullets and wanted to find something different to do with his time.

Ray had used our bullets in his 300 Weatherby on an Alaskan brown bear hunt. He found a guide to fly him in on a floatplane. They landed on the water and were making camp when Ray said to his guide, "How about me taking the cook and walking back a few miles to look at the country?" The guide said, "Be sure and take your guns."

So the cook took his 30–06 and Ray took his 300 Weatherby and they walked up a finger ridge. A lot of Kodiak's ridges run down towards the ocean about a quarter mile apart. On one of these ridges they saw a beautiful bear.

Ray stood transfixed, watching through his binoculars. The big silvertip walked in the sun along the top of the next ridge, about 300 yards away, long hair rippling in the wind. Ray and the cook started looking for a way to get a little closer to the bear so they could set up for a shot. Then the cook spotted another bear in the canyon and it was headed their way. Ray turned to look. It was coming uphill toward them and the cook said, "He'll get our scent pretty soon, then he'll turn around and run like crazy." The cook turned out to be better at cooking than at telling the future.

As Ray watched, the bear began to clack its jaws together, clearly agitated. With the wind at their backs, the bear had their scent now and he kept coming up the hill.

The cook was walking backward, calling on his deity to condemn the bear's maternal heritage to the eternal furnace.

Ray stood there with his 300 Weatherby and held the crosshairs right on the big bear's nose. When it was so close Ray could see it wasn't going to stop, he shot it and the bear dropped like it had been pushed out a window, twenty stories up.

Ray slammed the bear with another round from his Weatherby, turned around and hurried to catch up with the cook who already had a good head start. Back at camp, they found the guide and told him the big brown bear hunt was over and they'd better go back up the hill and skin out their trophy. The cook said he'd like to go back up and help, but he had to get dinner started.

Neither Ray nor the guide was happy, because the bear he had shot was not the one they were after. The bear they had seen on that far ridge had been much bigger, with a prettier coat.

John and Louise at the plant.

When they climbed back up the hill, the bear was gone. The guide followed the bear's tracks down the hill and they found him down in the creek bottom, very much alive, and madder than hell. They finished him off and when they started skinning the big beast found out why he had such a bad attitude. He had been shot about a week earlier and was very mad at anything that looked like a hunter.

It turned out that Ray's first shot had just grazed the top of the bear's head, yet it had knocked the bear clear over. If he had shot about a half–inch higher, he would have missed and the bear would have gotten him.

Ray came down to see me, we got to be good friends, and he said he wanted to join me in business.

I needed a partner who could handle the Cash and Sales Department. Ray didn't care much about making bullets, but he loved to hunt and he liked to sell. He got a kick out of being our sales manager and together we made and sold many bullets.

Ray also hunted deer in eastern Oregon. He had an area where he often found coal–black phase mule deer. He sometimes brought a black buck home. Often they

were not very big bucks, but that didn't matter to Ray. Once he took a forked horn deer to the taxidermist and when he brought it home, it was a four–point. It wore the same black cape but had different antlers.

Ray and I became good friends with a fellow we called KP who ran the hotel in Frenchglen. We came to know him well over the years. Ray loved the Steens too and he'd go over and stay with KP, ride horses and hunt. KP had a lovely, well–educated wife. The hotel thrived with her doing the cooking, while he managed it and pumped gas for their service station. But Mr. P quit looking at Mrs. P and spent too much time looking at the bottom of his whiskey glass. Mrs. P got mad and left.

KP's big thing in life was making whiskey. He made all kinds of stuff. He'd get a little drunk and say to himself, "I'm going to go out and shoot a deer." After this went on a while, the game warden began to get interested. Finally, KP shot a deer

John and Louise with a letter from a customer. The first advertisements and articles about the Nosler Partition sparked the imagination of shooters all over the world.

while the game warden was watching. When the warden approached, KP took a shot at him, too.

The first I heard about it, the police in Burns phoned and asked if I knew this fellow. "Yes," I said, "I know him real well." They asked, "Do you have a Weatherby rifle there?" I knew something was haywire so I said, "I may have several Weatherbys, but my partner and KP were doing a lot of hunting and trading around so I may have the gun and I may not. I don't know what you are really interested in finding out." I called Ray, and told him what had happened, and he came right over from Lake Oswego and found KP in jail. Which was a good place for him. They had his trial in Burns and Ray got him a lawyer. No one in Burns would convict him so he got out free and clear with the recommendation: "For God's sake, please don't shoot at any more game wardens." He behaved after that.

Ron, Louise and John Nosler in the front office at the plant in Bend, Oregon.

When Ray Wade became a partner, we also got several other Wade family members. Ray put together a coalition of Wades to buy a 51 percent position in our company. By himself, Ray didn't have a controlling interest, but with his family behind him, he had a 51 percent voting block.

Ray was suited to sales management and the business grew. I didn't know it at the time, but something was still missing. Something called marketing. We were growing but our lack of marketing expertise was holding us back.

For many years, Ray wanted to tour Europe with his family. He finally said, "John, I'm going to take my wife and kids to Europe and we are going to live over there." And they moved to Italy.

"Over the years, I had a lot of good employees and was fortunate to work with people who became my friends." – John Nosler

I had always wanted to get to know Norma, one of Europe's leading ammunition companies. I had sold them a few bullets, and I said, "Ray, go on up to Sweden and see those guys while you are in Europe." He did and got acquainted with the manager of Norma.

Norma manufactured all types of ammunition for sale in Europe and Africa. They had contacted us about using some of our Partitions in their ammunition. Ray hoped to get to know them and maybe sell some of our bullets.

Ray and Norma's president, Amend Enger, became good friends and later toured Europe together. Mr. Enger was sold on our bullets and Norma became an excellent outlet for us. 🦌

CHAPTER 19

Accuracy is a Frame of Mind

The Partitions were becoming popular. Our problem was that the tubing we used was expensive. We couldn't offer the bullets at a price that most sportsmen were willing to pay. One of the things that still bothered me was the all the scrap we wasted.

Since those early years, a lot has changed in the way we make our bullets. One thing that hasn't changed is the rigorous testing we put them through.

We have to shoot constantly to make sure the product we sell is consistent. When we are in the development stages of a bullet (and we're always working on something new), we are constantly shooting, testing, redesigning, and shooting some more. I wanted a shooting facility at the plant so someone lent us a backhoe and we dug a trench clear across and over the irrigation ditch and built an underground building 100 yards away. I bought a whole bunch of oil drums and welded them together, painted them with tar and buried them. This made an excellent tube and it wasn't very expensive. We crossed the ditch with those and then we had the tube from there on for the rest of it; about 10 or 15 yards was elevated after we crossed the ditch.

We also put a 500–gallon water tank in back of the plant. We would get up there and shoot into the water tank to test bullets. It was a beautiful way to do it. The other way was to make a long rack filled with newspapers. I soaked them in water and put them in a slot, left a one–inch space, then more newspaper and another space. The reason I had an inch space was because I wanted to see how the fragments of lead would penetrate the paper and how often and how deep they would still fragment. The front lead on the Partition bullets was exposed and I found out that it was a tremendous contributor to the fragmentation of the front of the bullet.

I was very interested in getting extrusion underway. I'd been thinking about it since the 1950s and I knew it was the only way we could make enough bullets to supply the growing demand.

To extrude means to shape a metal by forcing punches into it through a die. This was not being done in the United States prior to World War II and all our information on extruding came from the German engineers that we consulted with. I finally got a German book about it. The author set up different kinds of presses to do certain kinds of extruding. He was running a job shop, which I thought was tremendous. I gobbled up everything I could learn from him. Thank goodness the book was in English! It gave me an awful lot of encouragement.

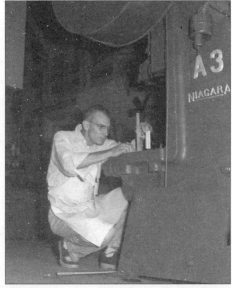

John Nosler (pictured here at right) built his reputation on an unwavering commitment to precision and accuracy..

The material comes in wire form and you have to shear it. Then you bump the sheared slug into as near of a perfect cylinder shape as you can. That goes to the annealing oven so all parts of it are as even–tempered as possible. We are very careful to make sure all our metal is uniform.

I tooled up to run some jackets extruded about halfway down. The rear would be solid copper. It looked like it would work so I decided to make a bullet with lead in the front and a solid metal rear. We called it the Zipedo.

The rear of the Zipedo was solid and the front of it had a lead core, enclosed by a thin jacket for rapid expansion. Rather than run the solid part through the rifling, I ran annular rings in it so the metal could flow back into the vacancy, and in fact

John with his rifle, spotting scope and shooting bench. Such field tests were indispensable in developing the bullets that sportsmen the world over could rely upon.

Fred Huntington (left) and
Bruce Hodgdon.

Les Bowman of Cody, Wyoming (left), and John Nosler.

Fred Huntington (left) and
John Nosler.

Fred and Barbara Huntington in Huntington's showroom in California.

I had to make them a little heavier because the bullet went through too easy. I was learning as I went along.

I bought another press and tooled it up to get the bigger press free so that I could tool it up for extruding. I bolted on heavy braces to keep it rigid for extruding. I developed extruding the jacket a little over halfway down. That was about as far as I could go on that equipment. We made them in 22s and 243s. They were excellent for penetration but they still didn't make a game bullet out of a 22. Our Zipedo bullet was a fun project that paved the way for the Solid Base and Ballistic Tip.

My friend Pat Metke was on the Game Commission for the State of Oregon and was also in the State Legislature and ran an insurance company. A lot of hunting and gun fanciers came to the Game Commission to try and make 22s legal for deer. The Game Commission was not very excited about it.

Pat called me to come up and speak to them. Some of the 22 game bullet boosters were there also. They were showing me how much steel you could shoot through with a 22 rather than an '06 and that wasn't at all new to me because I had already done all that stuff. So I said, "No, I don't think a 22 should be legal. Yeah, for a guy that has a lot of time to hunt and if he's a real good shot, but for the weekend hunter that more or less has to shoot if he sees something, I say no. I just can't endorse it."

They suggested I try my Zipedo bullet in a 22 on a deer and report back to them. "Sure," I said, "if you can guarantee I won't be arrested." "Just don't advertise it too much," they said.

I worked up some hot loads for my 225 Winchester and went to Snow Mountain where I had hunted many times before. I started out at the bottom and went right up the mountain. I hadn't gone 50 feet from my pickup and I could see deer over in the brush. "That's not work for a 22," I told myself and kept walking uphill and saw one walk out about 200 yards ahead of me. He trotted along and stopped. I thought I'd better be closer than that, so I didn't shoot.

Near the top of the mountain, I saw two identical bucks. I picked one of them, about 65 yards away. I had a good bead on it when I shot and knew pretty much where I'd hit it, but the deer didn't react in any visible manner. I knew that I *had* hit it and that I hit it good. I stood and let things settle down, then I walked up. At the spot where I had last seen the deer, I got down on my hands and knees and found deer tracks.

After following a little ways, I finally found one drop of blood. After another 30 yards of crawling on my knees in the heavy brush, I came up on my deer. That convinced me. I had made a good shot and he couldn't have lived very long and maybe should have dropped quicker but he didn't, so I went back and reported what I had done and left the decision up to them. I still don't think the 22 centerfire is a good caliber for deer.

I bought another big press and I set it up to extrude more Zipedos. I wanted to extrude the Partition, but I didn't dare try because I'd upset the manufacture. I

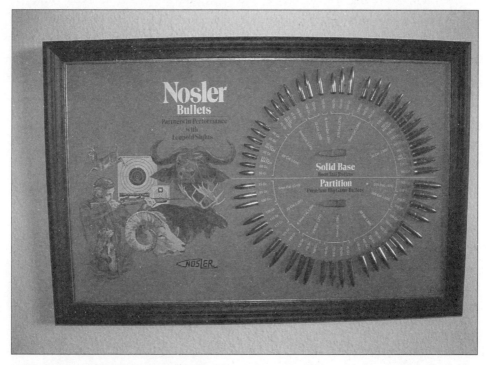

Nosler's fourth bullet board. The bullet boards became rather popular over the years and early ones are difficult to find.

tooled up this new press to make more Zipedos and found I needed more help in the shop.

Ed Neff was 25 years old when he came to work for us. He had good experience, having worked since he was 18 in a number of different machine shops. He already had a job, but he was looking for something different. Ed told me he could run any machine I had and any that I was going to have. I told him my only requirement was perfection.

I tried to give everybody who worked for me a challenge. We were doing some experimental work for the government at the time, building prototypes of a steel bullet. It had annular rings and grooves to allow the steel to flow under pressure. We didn't have an optical comparitor machine for precision measuring, but we had Ed Neff. He was young, had good eyes, and knew how to run a lathe. I told him, "Sharpen up a tool and I want you to cut four thousandths into the metal then move over the width of the thread and go four thousandths again." We were making a roller to roll the threads on that steel bullet. The reason for the threads was I didn't want to shoot the solid iron through the rifling. I wanted a valley for the metal to go down and relieve all the pressure.

I knew I was asking Ed to do something that I couldn't even do myself, but I kept telling him that he could do it. And he did. I had a device which I used to measure the depth and the work was perfect. And he did it on an ordinary lathe, with nothing but eyesight and a glass to look through and the dial on the lathe.

I got to know everybody in the company as well as I could because I trusted them with everything I had. Over the years, I had a lot of good employees and was fortunate to work with people who became my friends. Best of all was working with my two sons and my grandchildren. Bob and Ron both took time away and pursued other careers, but were ready to help when I (and Nosler Bullets) needed them.

Bob worked with us part–time during his high school years. He was a good athlete and I enjoyed watching his football games. Most of all, Bob loved to hunt and we hunted together as much as we could. But, like Ron before him, he had to go prove himself in the world outside Bend.

He investigated all branches of the military and chose to work in submarines if he could get in. He applied to the Navy and made it, then signed up for four years. He spent most of his career on the submarine USS Nathan Hale. There were two crews, the Blue and the Gold. They took turns at sea and would stay under for two months at a time. I was proud to see him serving our country, but hoped that one day he would come back to work with us. 🌾

CHAPTER 20

Getting It Right—Perfecting the Partition and Zipedo

I was always looking for ways to make our products better and our production more efficient. I would set up a machine to run several operations, then think about ways to perform more operations. I was never satisfied. I would puzzle on a problem for weeks or months, drawing at the drafting table or scribbling notes on a napkin. Sometimes I would stand in the shop and stare at a machine for a long time while my brain worked on the problem.

In the early 1960s there was very little information about how to take chamber pressures of the cartridges when they were fired. Since we were making a bullet that would be loaded by the customer, it would be handy to put out some method for him or her to take a chamber reading of the pressures that we had internally in the cartridge. So I thought about it a great deal and finally came up with a small–diameter disk of steel, a thin disk. I put an eighth of an inch flat indent about 1/10,000[the] an inch deep into the steel. I curved the thing, we put a little indent in the cartridge case, laid the steel disk in there, and closed the bolt on it. I finally found out how deep to make the indent to record, say, 50,000 pounds per square inch.

It was a very good way to detect pressure. We really needed it and we used it a great deal. I didn't market this pressure detector much, but we sold some of them. Later, computer software was developed and, of course, that made calculating pressure a lot easier.

After Roy Banta quit, we all had to pick up the slack. Ed and some of the others were working six days a week to keep up with orders for the Partition and work on

"I was always looking for ways to make our products better and our production run more efficient. I would set up a machine to run several operations, then think about ways to perform more operations. I was never satisfied. I would puzzle on a problem for weeks or months, drawing at the drafting table or scribbling notes on a napkin. Sometimes I would stand in the shop and stare at a machine for a long time while my brain worked on a problem." – John Nosler

the new projects. Everyone tested their own bullets and we all took turns shooting in the Ballistics Lab. Part of perfecting processes was finding the right people. Sometimes I had to find them; sometimes they found me. In the late 1960s, a young machinist named Alan Ashforth wandered into our plant. He had been working in the experimental tooling department for RocketDyne in Los Angeles. They gave him six weeks of vacation and he spent two weeks of it in central Oregon every year. I guess he was bored, because he asked if we would hire him.

Louise was working in the front office when he came in and asked to fill out an application. She went out in the shop and found me, and I interviewed him and showed him around. I wanted to know if he had a background in the shooting sports. He did. My next question: Was he a member of the National Rifle Association? He was.

John Nosler with one of his famous Partition bullets.

Every box of bullets was weighed to ensure proper count.

He told me that if I could draw something, he could build it. I handed him a blueprint of a trimmer arm that lifts the cutter up and down. I told him to build it. He went out in the shop, put on an apron and built it. I didn't know it at the time, but his wife was waiting outside in the camper. I gave him the job. Within a month he was living behind the shop in his camper while his wife sold their house in California.

He was a very meticulous person so I put him to work in the machine shop building Zipedos, then moved him into the grinding room to build equipment. He had a certain feel for machinery and tooling and his skills were quite an asset to our company.

One year Alan had been working very hard and had missed almost all of the deer season. Finally, with one day left in the season, he asked if he could take a day off. I

A nice Wyoming mule deer for Bob Nosler (left). "Field–testing our bullets has always been a part of what we do." – John Nosler

couldn't spare him, but I couldn't see him miss deer season either. I told him that he could take the day off and I would pay him for it if he brought in a buck.

He drove up to the Bear Wallows area west of town and bagged a forked horn mule deer. Before the workday was over, he was back at the plant. He backed his pickup right into the shop all the way to the front office wall, yarded the buck out of the truck, and headed for my office to show me. I stopped him before he made it to the front office and paid him for a day's work. 🦌

CHAPTER 21

To the Yukon for Moose, Caribou, and Grizzly

In 1968 Jack James, Francis Cheney, Tom Alley, and I drove the Alaska Highway to the Yukon line and met our guide. We were all very excited to be there again. Fran Cheney had a grizzly tag. We left our pickups at the end of the road and the outfitter flew us one at a time in his Piper Cub out to the log cabin he had built back in the wilderness. Ours was the first group to occupy the cabin and hunt this virgin territory.

When my turn came, he flew me around to get a look at the country. There was snow on the highest peaks and green trees and ridges below. I could see small meadows and runoff streams and little lakes in the timber. Good game country. Flying lower, we came on a great bull moose and circled low a couple of times to get a good look. He finally reared up and shook his big antlers, ready to fight. He didn't know what the hell was coming down to him, but he was ready to take it on. We saw a grizzly too. Finally we landed on the crude strip the guide had made, bumping along over rocks, and stubborn bushes that hadn't given way to the hoe.

We were greeted at the cabin by our guide, his wife (our cook), and their nine year–old son. Schools are few and far between in that country, so the boy was tutored by his mother. After talking with the boy, I guessed she was doing a mighty good job of it. Early in the season, the boy had killed his first moose. Moose meat was a big part of our menu for the next week. What we didn't know at the time was that a grizzly was also feeding on the same moose we were eating. The carcass was about a mile from camp along the trail we would ride out for the hunt.

The outfitter had hired an Indian he called Yukon Teddy and we had a lot of fun with him. Our outfitter told us, "For goodness sake, don't give Teddy any booze." A big pot of stew was on the stove and we were sitting down to eat when Yukon Teddy looked out the window. A great big bull moose had walked up next to the cabin, not more than 50 feet away. "One of you guys want to shoot a moose?" he asked. I looked up. It was a pretty darn good one. Francis, who always had trouble with his guns, wanted to shoot it. He had brought a new semi–automatic along for the hunt.

He brought it down to the plant once and wanted me to fix it. Hell, I didn't know what to do with it. The gun must have had a crooked barrel or something. Anyway, the best you could get with it was about a four–inch group.

Riding the river after a successful hunt. "There was snow on the highest peaks and green trees and long ridges below. Everywhere were small meadows and runoff streams. Good game country." – John Nosler

John Nosler on horseback. " A mile from camp we came on the boy's moose carcass and chased the grizzly off it."

Jack James with a Canada moose that fell to a Partition.

Tom Alley (left), Francis Cheney and Jack James arrive at camp.

The big moose had walked away, but was still less than 50 yards from us by the time Fran stood up, grabbed his case, found his ammunition, and loaded his rifle. Fran leaned against the doorjamb and commenced to empty his magazine, the spent cartridges kicking out into the garden.

The moose stood there looking around, as if wondering what all the noise meant. Finally he just walked away, fading back into the trees. The Indian said, to no one in particular, "Wouldn't you know that this is the sonofabitch with the grizzly tag?"

Going out the next morning on horses we came across the boy's moose carcass. We chased the grizzly off it as we were going out. The carcass was just getting ripe enough that the griz thought it smelled pretty good. The smell of bear had the horses spooked and it was all we could do to get them to pass the dead moose.

John and Yukon Teddy with John's moose, one of the best he ever took in Canada.

 Expanded Nosler Partition.

Francis and I decided to hunt together. He liked my gun a lot and knew he wasn't going to get anything with his gun so we stayed together. We spent over three hours that day watching caribou. There was one little band that stayed pretty close. All came back to the same spot and started feeding. Suddenly, one would rear up and look around and then the rest would too. One or two of them would take off like crazy and run out there a ways, look around and then trot back. They were very comical. Later in the day we watched a pair of foxes hunting marmots. We should have been hunting but we were having too much fun.

John with Francis Cheney's grizzly. The hunters surprised the bruin feeding on an old moose carcass. "Francis and I rode up and saw the bear standing beside the kill. Swinging out of the saddle, leaving his binoculars on a strap hanging from the saddle horn, Francis kept his hands on the reins. His horse started to buck like crazy. I yanked my rifle from the scabbard and threw it to Francis. I remember looking up in the air and I could see his field glasses about ten feet higher than his horse." – John Nosler

We climbed up on a high ridge and from our viewpoint counted 27 moose all within easy distance. One or two of the moose were very good, with racks over 60 inches wide. We didn't shoot a caribou or a moose that day, but still had a few days left to hunt.

When the guide brought our horses about the mid–afternoon we started back to the cabin. The guide was on a good horse and we were riding the slow stock. We couldn't kick them hard enough to move faster than a slow walk. I told Francis,

This was a day for hunting caribou. With all four hunters and their guides together, they found the herd and several good bulls. Francis Cheney (right) poses with his guide and a nice bull.

John Nosler holds the horse, while the guide tightens the cinch for the pack back to base camp.

"You're the one with a grizzly tag. Better get up there with that guide or you won't get a chance to use it. I'll beat on your horse from the rear and you can beat on him from the top and maybe you can keep up with the guide, because that grizzly will be back working that kill."

I knew damn well that he would. Francis agreed but we never could catch that guide; he stayed a hundred yards ahead of us all the time. We got to the moose and sure enough the grizz was there. Our guide's horse became unruly and he couldn't

"Packing out Francis Cheney's moose, this horse slipped on the steep trail and began to buck and kick. The pack slipped around and the moose horns could have gutted the poor thing, but finally it stopped bucking and we were able to cut the pack loose and re–rig it." – John Nosler

hold it. Before he could jump out of the saddle, the horse whirled and pounded away.

Francis and I rode up and saw the bear standing beside the kill. Swinging out of the saddle, leaving his binoculars on a strap hanging from the saddle horn, Francis kept his hands on the reins. His horse started to buck like crazy. I yanked my rifle from the scabbard and threw it to Francis. I remember looking up in the air and I could see his field glasses about ten feet higher than his horse.

Fran started shooting at the grizzly, putting the bullets in his gun one at a time instead of loading them in the magazine. He shot and shot until he was out of ammo. With one shot, he nicked the bear while it was going uphill, and that's the worst thing to do because they can come back downhill faster than you can imagine. The guide finally got his horse under control and galloped back and said "You guys get in the saddle and get the hell out of here. That grizz will get you way before you get him." We obeyed, caught Francis's horse and hit the trail, heading for the cabin.

Jack and Tom had been hunting together that day. Jack shot a caribou. Tom was after a moose and hadn't seen an opportunity yet. Teddy was outside seeing to the horses so we each had a couple of drinks before he came back in.

The next day we were all together, walking along the high side of a ridge. After a while we spotted the grizzly about 300 yards away. We dismounted and Francis took a rest on a rock. Francis either had my gun or was using Jack James's, I can't remember now, but with his very first shot he hit that grizzly in the foot and I never could figure out how the hell he managed that. The bigger surprise was that he hit it again in the neck and down went the bear. Later that day we all shot our caribou and the guys that wanted a moose got their moose. I shot a very good one.

That evening we were having a drink with the guide and his wife when Teddy walked in. He was furious. "What? You think I'm not good enough to drink with you?" he stormed. "Well, I'll tell you what. Then I'm not good enough to help you load up your meat either, or ride your damn horses out to the road." That said, he stomped out, leaving us speechless. We all agreed that the thing to do was give him a reasonable amount to drink so we did and put the bottle away where he wouldn't find it later.

Waiting for the plane. "I had the honor of flying out with the grizzly skin. My horns were tied on the wings and Francis Cheney's bear rug was on my lap. I told the pilot to fly that plane as fast as he could, because I was afraid I was going to throw up." – John Nosler

The next day we were going out to skin the bear and I said, "Better take a bottle of Scotch because we'll never be able to skin that damn bear sober. He'll stink to high heaven." We didn't have any trouble finding where we'd left the bear. There was no way to not find him because he stunk so bad we just followed the scent right to him. We each took turns skinning and skinned as long as we could until we were ready to vomit. There's no way to describe how bad those things smell after they've been working on a rotten moose for a week. But we finally got the bear skinned and had to leave.

I had the honor of flying out with the grizzly skin. My horns were tied on the wings, and Francis Cheney's bear rug was on my lap, and the pilot was right in front of me—no room for anything else. Off we went and I told the pilot to fly that plane as fast as he could because I was afraid I was going to throw up.

We landed on the Alaska Highway and the outfitter's wife was waiting there with a big Chevy Suburban. I took a deep breath of fresh air, glad to have some distance between me and that bearskin and that little airplane.

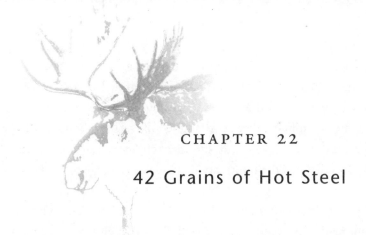

CHAPTER 22

42 Grains of Hot Steel

With all of our technical knowledge and our manufacturing ability, I thought that we might be able to do a little work for the government. I contacted the Governor's office and asked how to get a bid for the Federal government. He said he didn't know how to do it and none of his people knew how either. "Why don't you go down and find out and we'll pay your way," he suggested. He loaned me a nice young guy from his office as an escort.

First, we visited the Navy. They seemed very glad to see us. In their minds we represented the State of Oregon and they were very intent on showing us how to bid on their projects. They were really hurting for bids, because they didn't seem to get the information out to the right people. They'd end up hiring the parts made as if there was no bid at all. I wanted to find out if we could work with them and make a little money in the process.

We visited the Army next, and met with a colonel and his staff who told us how to apply for an Army bid. That consumed quite a bit of the day and we were still supposed to meet with the Air Force. We fooled them and said we would like to meet with them that afternoon and might be a little bit late because we would have to find the place. We rented a car and took off as fast as we could to try and get over to Sacramento.

It was after 6 p.m. by the time we got there but they kept the base open for us and threw out the red carpet. We were very important to them, I guess. We were representing the State of Oregon, so they gave us the same type of information on how to apply for Air Force contracts.

Back home, we took all the information and I thought I was going to apply to work on manufacturing a hinge for one of the Air Force airplanes. It wasn't a very big deal but I just wanted to get started on it. So I made out my application and sent it in. They called me and told me that I had omitted the section about how I was going to package this thing. I was amazed. But they told me to call a library in one of the southern states that had the information on how to package to Air Force requirements.

It took a great deal of talking to convey to them exactly what I needed, so by the time I got the information the bidding was closed. Even though I didn't apply for any more, I knew how and I sent the information on all of the service branches back to the Governor's office. I'm sure it did help Oregon businesses a great deal for the factories that needed work to keep them busy. Government work was very good once you knew how to get it.

But something else interested me more than building obscure parts for airplanes. The government shot away a lot of bullets during the World Wars, Korea, and the Vietnam War. All the bullets that were being fired by the military all over the world had consumed a tremendous amount of copper. I had some ideas on a steel bullet and so I got in touch with the Aberdeen Proving Grounds military operation. I said

John Nosler at his drafting table, working through the intricacies of another manufacturing challenge.

I was interested in building a steel bullet to relieve some of the copper stocks being mined.

They were intrigued. In a week they sent the FBI out to fingerprint and to get our background data. Then they sent their engineers out to see us. I had already made a number of steel bullets in 22 caliber. And being made out of steel, to the exact same proportions as the copper/lead bullet, the steel bullet weighed 42 grains. The government engineers were very interested in the way that I had formed the steel. I think they had tried it a number of times and the forming pressures had become very high, trying to push the steel up through into the sharp point that they wanted. I had conquered that part and they became more and more interested in the project.

I made a number of samples and I put a thin bronze plating over the steel to make a cushion between the steel bullet and the steel barrel. It seemed to work quite well. Then they came back with a 55–grain bullet with a very high ballistic coefficient; it was a long skinny thing. I figured out a way to press that thing on a little 15–ton press. The engineers were absolutely amazed because they had other companies try to form that without success. Of course, I had a lot of experience by that time and was able to do it.

John Nosler and Jack James on a fall elk hunt.

John's striped marlin clearing the water. Next to hunting and shooting, fishing is one of John's favorite pastimes.

Our partnership with Ray Wade had been a good one. Since 1958 we had grown from 6 to 20 employees and our production was up. I had seen it coming for awhile. Ray wanted out of the bullet business. He came home from Europe and told me he had lost interest in the bullet business. "I think I'd like to sell my interest, John. Would you like to buy it?" I said I would, but that I had a very strong suspicion that Leupold and Stevens would like to become associated with us.

Over the years, I had come to know Marcus Leupold and Jack Slack of Leupold and Stevens quite well. We talked with Marcus Leupold, Jack Slack, and the rest of their management team. The deal was made. Leupold and Stevens would take over as our partners. I was excited about the opportunity to buy the equipment we needed and use the marketing power of Leupold and Stevens to introduce our bullets to more of the shooting public. 🦌

John in the fighting chair

CHAPTER 23

Copper, Computers, and Chronographs in the Corporate World

The Wades sold their 51% ownership in 1969 and Nosler Bullets Inc. became a subsidiary of Leupold and Stevens. We had good partners up to this point. Now we had a great partnership.

It was Leupold & Stevens who helped finance the extrusion process for the Partition bullet. I had many of hundreds of thousands of dollars invested before I made the first Partition bullet by extrusion and I was getting kind of jumpy. But I said, by God, I can do it. We bought three 60–ton Bliss punch presses and I converted them into transfer presses with ejectors. They are still running and will be for another 100 years.

For years we had been trying to forge an alliance with one of the major ammunition manufacturers to get them to use our bullets in their products. Through the partnership with Leupold and Stevens, we were finally successful. Federal was the first. Now, a whole generation of shooters has grown up shooting Nosler bullets loaded in their premium ammunition.

What a change. All of a sudden Nosler Bullets was a legitimate player in the shooting sports industry. We were no longer just a little company trying to sell a product that was different. All of a sudden we were a company selling a proven, established product. All of a sudden... after 22 years.

There are partners and there are the *right* partners. Don O'Bleness was a good partner. Ray Wade was a good partner. But Leupold and Stevens was the right partner to grow the business. They had the capital and the dream and vision to position a business in the eyes of the industry and the consumer. They had people who were professional shooting sports marketers. They had a much stronger understanding of how to get the product into the distribution system. They knew the writers and knew how to get articles written about the product, articles that the shooting public would read.

Look at any old *American Rifleman* magazine from about 1969 to 1985. It was uncommon to see a cover that did not include a picture of a rifle with a Leupold scope. That was the kind of marketing power we were partnered with. They really understood how to help us.

Here was our tiny little shop hitched to their big company. We had almost 20 employees when we were at peak production and they had over 200 employees at the time, dragging us around, teaching us how to grow. We were able to move into a new building, add new products and market and sell them. Because we had the right partner.

Snow can be a boon on an elk hunt. John Nosler with a bull he took in Oregon.

Now our business was marching forward. But it had waited 22 years to start marching. All this time, it had been waiting for the *right* marching partner.

From the time he was a teenager, Ron was a very big help in the bullet business. He grew up in the Ashland schools in southern Oregon and so it was natural for him to attend Southern Oregon College. He majored in English and worked in our sales department, in the front office, and in Personnel for many years, retiring in 2003.

Bob was out of the Navy after four years. I didn't want to tell him to come and join me in business. I wanted to see him make his own decision. He finally did and said, "Dad, I hear more and more about your bullet business and the work that you're doing and a lot of people say 'Why don't you join your dad? He's got something going there.' So I would like to." And we've been very close ever since.

Bob was itching to go hunting now that he was a civilian again. I was busy with a few projects, including finding the funds to build new schools in our school district. The school board was considering appointing me to the budget committee. Still,

Roger Roberts (foreground) and Bob Nosler with a nice mule deer buck Roberts tagged on a Wyoming hunt.

there is always time for hunting and Bob and I were looking forward to spending some time together.

We were with four other buddies to hunt mule deer and pronghorns on a large well–run ranch. The son of the rancher was to guide Bob and me. Bob had not shot a pronghorn before, but had a number of deer to his credit before his enlistment in the Navy. We had a few chances but Bob passed them up, wanting a pretty good trophy if we could make contact.

With the rest of our party hunting the same ranch, it wasn't long before the herds were pretty spooked. The second day, Bob and I crawled over a big hump to view two nice bucks with some does. We estimated they were something like 250 yards away. Bob laid down in the Montana cactus to get a good rest on his backpack. He pulled his 7 mm Remington Magnum tight against his shoulder and squeezed. It was a nice shot. The pronghorn fell and Bob had his trophy.

Since I was an old–timer with several nice heads at home, I was not worried about getting another antelope, but I guessed I would try.

Now the animals were very spooked. The next morning, Bob and the ranch owner's son and I were sitting on a knoll overlooking a large area. From far away, we saw a herd running directly toward us. I was lying down with a rock as a rifle rest, hoping the antelope would come close enough to shoot. Instead, at about 600 yards, they turned at a right angle. Bob and our guide were watching with field glasses. Both said the lead one had a good set of horns. I had a good rest so I thought I would shoot to make them run faster. I led the lead buck by six antelope body lengths and held up six high and shot. I could hardly believe my eyes. The lead one went down.

We paced off the distance as we walked. When we got there, there were two dead bucks, lying about a foot apart. None of us at that distance could see there were two running together in the lead. Both of them, now very dead. I was using my 270 with 150–grain Partitions.

I phoned Louise that night and told her what I had done and joked that I would probably be put in jail because my tag called for only one antelope. When I got home, she said she nearly fainted because she had seen my name in the local paper under the headline, "John Nosler gets two years." I had been appointed to the school budget board for a two–year term.

Jack Slack, from Leupold and Stevens, was our sales manager. We hunted rockchucks a great deal together. Jack loved it so much that he looked for some property of his own so he could shoot 'chucks anytime he wanted to. He found a good spot north of Redmond a ways and leased the ground from the guy who owned it. The fellow could run his stock while he wasn't there, but Jack would phone him and say he was coming the next week and the guy would clear his cattle out of there. I went with him an awful lot.

The property had two rock walls, one about 100 yards according to my rangefinder and the next one around 375 yards. We put our bedrolls down on the canvas and once you get sighted in with a good gun you can't miss. Then we'd go to the farther one and get sighted in right on the money, and we'd shoot a bunch of those big old chucks.

John Nosler with a four–point mule deer buck while testing bullets in Wyoming.

Old Jack was a good shot too. He later went to Africa with a 30–06 and 165–grain Nosler Partitions and shot a lot of the antelope and other game. Said he never had to use another shot if he did it right.

In 1972, I changed the Zipedo bullet into a nearly full–jacket extrusion and we renamed it the Solid Base. The Partition jacket was extruded, and both bullets were made from 95% copper and 5% zinc wire. The slugs were hopper–fed into the presses, extruded with no scrap and with much cheaper material, making much–improved bullets.

In 1973 I met a young engineer who would eventually make a big difference in our company. Bill Lewis had graduated from Portland State University in 1971 with a degree in Mechanical Engineering. We were hoping to move to a new building and I thought I might have room for him. Ron had interviewed Bill and thought he could help us out with writing our first loading manual, engineering and ballistics. I told him I would try him for a week. Then Leupold and Stevens put our new building plans on hold and I had to tell Bill Lewis goodbye. Fortunately for us, we would see him again in the future.

Gail Root started working at Nosler in 1973. He had been working for Boeing as a draftsman. He was very valuable for us in the engineering department. He worked for us for over 25 years. I could start the drawings, then hand them over to him and he'd finish them and save me an awful lot of time.

We met Chub Eastman through our relationship with Leupold. He was from Montana, and was an accomplished hunter. He was working for Winchester. He did very well with them and Jack Slack of Leupold got acquainted with Chub and hired him away.

He did very well for Leupold. He was a tremendous benefit because he loved to hunt. What he brought to Leupold was the idea that, to be successful, you needed to do a lot of hunting trips with outdoor writers and make sure that their stories contained references to Partition bullets and Gold Ring scopes.

I don't know how many buffalo he shot over the years, but I know the last time he was in Africa with a broken leg, he shot two. He has bagged several grizzly bears. Everybody knows him and he knows everybody. I just love being over there hunting in Wyoming. We'll have people from other industries and Chub just gets up and takes over and everyone crowds around to hear his stories. Bob and Chub became good friends and went on a number of hunts together.

We were running out of room in the old plant and the place was getting real jammed up. My friend Bill Smith came to our rescue and introduced us to the land we are on now. Bill knew an industrial builder from California. He brought this fellow up and introduced him to us and we made an agreement that he would put up our building.

Before the building was constructed, we installed two four–foot–diameter tubes, 100 yards long, under the building. We have a large area set up at the far end with bullet traps to stop the bullets and keep the lead from penetrating into the soil. In the firing room we installed two chronographs, one for each tube. The chronographs record the velocity, the ballistic coefficient, group size, and the chamber pressure from the computer.

Visiting RCBS in Oroville California, 1969. From left: Fred Huntington, Bruce Hodgdon, Ray Speer, Jean Speer, Sonja Cheney, Arlan Cheney, Ron Nosler, Louise Nosler, John Nosler.

For the greatest consistency, we shoot from machine rests rather than using shoulder–fired rifles. This system eliminates operator error. A large number of rifle barrels are on hand, ready to fit into the machine rests. For further testing capability, we also have many regular hunting rifles at our disposal.

All Nosler bullets are inspected visually. Bullets are fed onto an endless belt, which rotates the bullets in view of the inspectors. Wearing white cotton gloves, the inspectors pick out the bullets with tarnish or scratches to ensure that the shooter is only sold the highest quality product.

All during the manufacturing process, sample bullets are taken from each finish press and tested for accuracy. If they don't shoot to our standards, the tester shuts that production line down until accuracy is restored.

We hired Bill Lewis in 1981. He had come over to the shop one day and was talking to Bob about targets, shooting, and reloading. Bob asked if he knew of any good engineers who might want to go to work for Nosler. Bill thought about it for half a second. "I sure do," he said. "Me."

I put Bill to work in the engineering office with me. It was a little cramped with two people but we made it work, sharing two drafting tables and a desk. It was odd at first, having someone to bounce ideas off of. I worked by feel and he worked by engineering theory and manufacturing procedure. I gave him the 200–grain 8 mm Partition for his first project.

I always believed that for best penetration and expansion you wanted to build a bullet that would shed 20–35% of its weight in fragmentation. You need some loss for best penetration and some fragmentation for optimum killing power.

Bill started with us in the days before Computer Aided Design and Drafting (CADD). We drew our bullets on paper at 10x scale. So Bill produced a new bullet based on his calculations. I approved his drawings and we built the bullet, then cut one in cross–section. I felt we needed more wall thickness to make it right. Bill took it back to the drawing board and we made another batch of 8 mm bullets. They worked.

Bill Lewis was a product of the computer age. He used a calculator. I used a pencil. Sometimes Bill would hand me a calculator. I always put it back on his desk. Longhand just felt better. I still don't like to use a calculator.

Soon after Bill came to work with us, we took a trip to Connecticut to learn more about transfer presses. Bill showed up at the house and Louise gave him our airline tickets and we set off for the Portland Airport with Bill driving my pickup. We arrived in Hartford, Connecticut, late at night minus our baggage.

We visited shops doing copper drawing, making tubes to hold ink in ballpoint pens and other such projects. We learned that German copper was better for extrusion than American copper because the Germans refined it better.

We learned a lot about transfer presses, which pleased me very much because we would later build some of our own from other types of presses and convert them. We also did some research for Leupold and Stevens in forming their scope by hammer forging. You would take an aluminum tube and put it on a certain type of a mandrel whichever shape you wanted and the machine would hammer from all directions and form the metal into shape. They never adopted the program because they thought it wouldn't fit in with the rest of their processes, but it was very valuable information. We came back with two different hammer–forging companies and they did do some corresponding.

In Hartford we drove by the Winchester plant. There was concertina wire all around the parking lot. Looked like a rough neighborhood. I was glad that we lived in little old Bend, Oregon.

We also visited the Platarg sales office. They had a couple Platargs on sale so I got interested in that press and Louise and I decided to go to England and do a little more investigating. I got well acquainted with those people in London. They had a beautiful plant and a lot of late–model equipment in it. I was very happy to have discovered the thing. I got all the info from them and came back and we all agreed that I had picked the right size. They priced it out as $150,000, so we held a meeting and decided to purchase it.

Louise and I went back over. It was an awful lot of fun for us to go over there because the press manufacturer took good care of us. He put us up in the best hotels, and wined us and dined us.

Platarg's Andrew Biem drove us around London, showing us the sights one afternoon. Louise was impressed with Andrew's car and asked what kind it was. Andrew pulled over to the side of the road, stopped and opened her door, bringing us up to the front of the car. He opened the hood and pointed to a badge on the engine. It was a Rolls Royce.

Platarg had the press all made up just as I had designed it. I took a bunch of bullet jackets over and we turned over the press by hand and let each operation work and it satisfied me perfectly. It would take an awful lot of time for it to come by ship to the United States so we had the thing flown to New York. I can imagine that big thing in an airplane. It has worked fine ever since. About that time I found a used one and we're using it a lot now, as well. Both of those Platargs work beautifully. Bill was a great help; he was in on everything and he and I worked together very well. I like him very much and these days I get to have lunch with him every once in a while.

While in London we decided to visit France, as Louise had not been there since she was a child. As we were waiting for a plane in Heathrow Airport, a man came up to me and asked in an Australian accent if I was John Nosler. He had recognized me from a picture in our loading manual.

CHAPTER 24

The Ballistic Tip

Early in the 1980s I began looking at ways to update our Solid Base product. I thought if I could put some sort of special tip on it, that it would be something that everybody would love to have. I couldn't quit thinking about this idea, so I started talking to Leupold and Stevens about it.

Around the same time, Bob and I began to look at ways that we could buy Leupold's shares back. In 1985, Bob put together a proposal but it didn't fly. Leupold backed off trying to sell, and put a few more years into making our product position stronger.

I dreamed up different types of tips on the drawing board and looked at them over and over again. I had enough experience by then that I was very aware of the weight placement in the bullet. You had to have a certain length and a certain amount of weight, and it had to be rearward. Hollow points were never satisfactory for hunting because the public never accepted them.

The European ammunition maker, Norma, had put a plastic tip in one of their bullets, a round ball, and closed the jacket around it. It was something that wouldn't batter in the magazine. I thought, why not make a real sharp, good–looking tip? I thought that a plastic tip would be attractive, appealing, and give spectacular performance.

I always liked the Remington Bronze Point bullet but found it to be less consistent than I wanted. The problem with the bronze point was that it was too heavy. If you are going to bring out the ultimate accuracy in a bullet, you need to have a light tip, and the bullet has to be longer, with the weight in the back. So that

John, varmint hunting in Central Oregon. "The off–hand position and the sitting position are the two most useful positions for the hunter. Spend time shooting both ways in practice."
– John Nosler

"The caliber of rifle you choose should fit you as well as the game you're after. It is much better to hit the game animal in the right place, with a rifle you can shoot well, than to hit it poorly with a large caliber rifle."
– John Nosler

John and Bob with a nice Wyoming pronghorn that fell to a prototype Ballistic Tip.

was the reason for the plastic. I was quite sure there was some kind of plastic that could stand up to that tremendous jolt.

Jack Slack brought me a sample of a plastic–tipped bullet that he had found in Canada. We examined it and felt we could improve on it.

I looked at using a conical point, with a beveled seat and column base. Bill Lewis suggested we put shoulders on it. That made sense to me. The next chore was figuring out how to feed it in the manufacturing process.

We made bullets, stuck plastic tips in them and they came out beautiful. Gail Root went to work shooting them in the Ballistics Lab. Someone in our group said, "let's color code them for caliber." Another great idea. Yellow for 270s. Green for 30s. Red for 7mm. When I got some made and gave a few away, everyone raved about them and wanted more.

I wanted to try out our new Ballistic Tips on game. Jack Slack suggested that we try them out at his place north of Redmond. We spread out a huge tarp, put down our bed rolls, and laid there in perfect ease. We had a big rock wall at a 100 yards, another at 400 yards and two smaller rock piles in between.

Jack and I had shot all morning, so we stopped to eat lunch and drink some coffee. I looked at the far rock wall and there was a magpie out there eating on a dead rockchuck. Jack asked, "Do you think you can hit him?" I said, "I don't know, I sure can try." I bet him dinner that night that I would hit the bird. I was shooting a 22–250 with a heavy match grade barrel, and a good 16–power Leupold scope. I

Roger Roberts (left) with John and Bob testing bullets in Wyoming.

took my time and took the slack out of the trigger. Boy did the feathers fly. Jack said, "All right there's another one coming up there." I said, "All right, this one's for the drinks." I got them both.

We introduced the Ballistic Tips with an ad in some magazines and sent some samples to gun writers and distributors. Shooters went hog wild for them. I was a little worried though, the jacket was a little thinner, with the tip causing rapid expansion. We had to do a little thickening of the jacket on a few calibers.

We brought the new Ballistic Tips and my 7mm Magnum on a combination antelope and deer hunt. With Bob and the guide, there were three of us in the pickup. We came up over a hill and a herd of antelope fell in beside us, running alongside like they do sometimes.

We stopped the truck and parked off the road. I leaned over the hood and shot. Down went my buck, but then he popped right back up. I know I hit him well, but I had to hit him again and down he went again. I was not pleased.

Colonel Charles Askins (left) and John discussing the finer points of bullet construction on a tour of the bullet plant in Bend, Oregon.

I guessed that the bullets were too explosive and exploded on contact at 3000 feet per second. I spent the rest of that trip shooting. I wanted to really test those bullets.

On another hunt Bob spotted a buck about 460 yards away. I sat down and took a careful rest, squeezed the trigger, and he dropped in his tracks. The bullet had slowed down enough that it was in its capacity.

We had to correct for the rapid expansion by thickening up the tip and, thank goodness we didn't sell very many before we got it right. Now our 7mm Ballistic Tips are well–respected products and probably go on more pronghorn hunts than any other bullet.

CHAPTER 25

Into Handgunning and Muzzleloading

While we were still in the design process on the Ballistic Tip we began work on a handgun project. The Partitions were extremely popular by this time and the Solid Base was selling well, but some stores weren't stocking our products because we didn't carry a full line. "Start making handgun bullets," they told us, "and we'll give you more space on our shelves."

Bullet designers across the industry have always struggled to find a bullet that will perform equally well through a wide range of velocities. A bullet that is tough enough to hold together at 15 yards will often not open at long range. Most handgun bullets only perform within a narrow velocity range, sometimes as small as 300 fps. We knew a little bit about fixing that type of problem. Why not produce a line of premium handgun and muzzleloader bullets?

In Engineering, we divided our time between Ballistic Tip development, handgun bullet work, and the normal process and tooling concerns that went with our every day production. We developed the pistol press to produce cup–and–draw bullets for handguns, starting with the 38 caliber products first.

In 1986 we brought our handgun products to the marketplace. Now we felt like we had a full line of products. The distributors, wholesalers, and retailers seemed to agree.

The cup–and–draw manufacturing process produces bullets that are satisfactory performers at the low end of the velocity scale. Shooters of higher velocity rounds, we felt, would be better served by a bullet that controlled expansion like our Partition. From the very beginning of our foray into the world of handgunning, I felt that we should develop a Partition handgun product. We set Engineering on

With the growing interest in modern muzzleloading, Nosler developed a line of products to serve this growing segment of the sporting public.

course to do that after we had a full line of centerfire handgun rounds in production. In 1998, working with engineers from Winchester, we developed Partition HG to the acclaim of handgun hunters everywhere.

With the growing interest in muzzleloading, and the development of modern in–line muzzleloading hunting tools, we developed a line of products out of our handgun line that would serve this growing segment of sportsmen. In hunting situations, muzzleloading bullets are shot at similar velocities and distances as high–power handguns. We went back to the plastics industry to marry our modern handgun bullets to muzzleloading rifles with a sabot.

A sabot is a plastic vehicle that carries a smaller bullet through the rifling of a muzzleloading rifle. The concave base of the sabot contains the pressure in the chamber as the sabot and bullet are propelled by the gunpowder's burning gases. The sabot falls away upon exit from the barrel. Using 44 or 45 caliber bullets in a 50– or 54–caliber barrel, we are able to achieve greater velocity and, dependent upon the twist of the barrel, greater accuracy. Our S.H.O.T.S. product is popular among target shooters and small game hunters. Our Partition HG sabots are the right products for any muzzleloader who is seeking the ultimate big game bullet.

"The first time I
hunted goats, the
weather happened
to be very mild and
clear. We had a
terrible time judging
the distance to the
goat I wanted. I
took careful aim
and squeezed the
trigger. The bullet
hit somewhat short.
We had guessed he
was 150 yards away.
In fact, he was over
300 yards from us."
– John Nosler

CHAPTER 26

Back to BC—
Roughing it in the Rockies

In the fall of 1987, we hunted in British Columbia again. Chub Eastman and my son Bob researched the top outfitters and regions, finally settling on the Musqwa River area, southwest of Fort Nelson. Elk and moose seasons ran concurrently, giving us the opportunity to take one or the other, or both. Chub and Bob chose Big 9 Outfitters, owned and operated by Olive Powell. Their allotment covered 1500 square miles of the Musqwa River drainage in the Rockies, accessible only by bush plane or a four–day horseback ride from the Alaskan Highway.

Bill Board, head of Quality Control and Ballistics for Federal Cartridge Corporation, accompanied Chub, Bob, and myself on our hunt. Bill was hoping to try out some of that Federal Premium ammunition on a bull moose. This would be his first hunt for either elk or moose.

Chub met us at Sea–Tac Airport in Seattle, driving "Big Blue," his 1975 F250 Ford 4x4. We were headed to BC by pickup, just like the old days, only better. This time I didn't have to drive.

We hit Chilliwack in BC, around eight o'clock in the evening then started again at ten o'clock the next morning. We stopped for fuel at Williams Lake. When I first saw this country 40 years ago, there had been only three buildings here. Now it was a thriving community, home to thousands. We drove that day until we hit Prince George, late in the evening. Fort St. John was our target for tomorrow.

Much of the country still looked like it did when I first saw it. Trees lined the highway, mule deer fed along the edge of the timber, a cow moose peered at us over the willows, and flights of geese scribed Vs in the autumn sky.

"On the ride downriver, we saw moose: young bulls, cows and calves. There were elk grazing on many of the open hillside meadows." – John Nosler

Much as I enjoyed the drive, I was looking forward to climbing in the bush plane. I love the sound of those old bush planes, the way they sputter as the prop catches the air, the slam of that aluminum door, the crackle of the radio, and the way the wind buffets the cabin and sends searching fingers inside. From the air, we feasted our eyes on thousands of acres of stunted firs and twisted hemlocks, soggy muskeg and snow on the tops of the mountains.

The plane taxied right to the front door of Big 9 Outfitters main lodge. The lodge was constructed of logs, and looked like there would be plenty of room for everyone. The stock in the corral looked healthy and fit. It was good to be here, if only for a little while. We would head to a downriver camp in the morning.

A good guide is always interested in whether or not his client can shoot. Part of the ritual of a guided hunt is the "sighting–in" session. Beware if your guide doesn't check to see if you can shoot. For our trip, we had brought a total of 12 rifles. Each was mounted with a Leupold Gold Ring scope. Stacked next to the rifles was a box of Federal Premium ammunition loaded with Nosler Partitions. Everyone could shoot.

On the ride downriver, we saw moose: young bulls, cows and calves. There were elk grazing on many of the open hillside meadows. Camp consisted of a log house, cook house, and two bunkhouses. Jill Wright, our cook, was making bread and cake when we arrived.

71 year–old Omar was the guide assigned to me. Doug London, an ex–rodeo bull rider, would be Bob's guide. We made a short hunt that afternoon and saw a pair of small six–point bulls. Since it was the first day, and dinner was on, we decided not to pursue them.

The next morning broke clear and cold. We loaded our rifles and mounted up, heading our separate ways, our breath turning to vapor in the frosty air. We saw elk and moose on the sidehills, looking them over, hoping for a good one. Back at camp, we saw a broad smile on Bill's face. He had taken his first moose. With a Nosler Partition bullet. His meat was still waiting for pickup out on the mountain.

The next day started off a little later because the wrangler couldn't catch all the horses before daylight. Bob headed off with Doug and Bill's guide, Blair, hoping to get a look at another bull that had been with the one Bill shot. No luck.

The fog was thick the next morning, with a solid curtain 500 feet above camp. Visibility was limited but the air held promise. I dressed extra warm because I knew Omar wanted to glass his favorite crossing all day long. Ever optimistic, Bob was smiling when we headed our separate ways. Doug was taking him to one of his favorite spots.

We watched Omar's crossing all day long, but didn't find a bull to shoot. Snow started falling in the afternoon and I was glad to get back to camp at dark.

Chub was the hero at dinner that night. One 210–grain Partition had anchored his 5x5 bull.

John Nosler at hunting camp.

John Nosler with the elk he took with a Partition bullet at 250 yards.

Chub was the hero in the morning as well. But for a different reason. We were all gathered at the corral, making sure lunch was in the saddlebags, checking our rifles, and mounting up. Chub liked to look at a grassy area that was visible from camp. We saw cows there from time to time. But this time, Chub spotted bulls through his binoculars. We bailed out of our saddles and glassed the bulls ourselves. One looked to be a 6x6, another was a 6x5, and a third was a 5x5. The smaller bulls were locked in a sparring match. I had never seen so many big bulls together before.

Doug, looking through his spotting scope, decided at least two were worth going after. Omar and I, and Bob and Doug started for the hill. It took us a while to get there, but we made it after a difficult stalk, keeping the wind in our faces. Finally, Bob and I were close, Doug and Omar right behind us. The elk had been bedded, but now the 5x5 stood to his feet and stared down the hill in our direction. 20 seconds later, the large 6x6 stood up, looking at us. The elk were 350 yards away and ready to run. Because of the slope of the terrain, we couldn't take a rest. We would have to stand and shoot them.

Bob shot first. His Winchester Model 70 .270 cracked as we heard the bullet strike and saw the bull buckle. Bob shot a second time, making another good shot. I brought my .338 Winchester up, found the 5x5 in my scope, and squeezed.

Hit hard, my bull was headed for the top of the ridge, but one more bullet ended his climb. He put his head down and started to slide backward, downhill. Back first, then head first, then end over end, he slid for at least 200 yards, coming to rest against a fallen tree. One shot had taken him in the shoulder, another in the boiler room.

There were a lot of smiles in the bunkhouse that night as Bill had ended his hunt with a good 6x6 bull elk.

The next day was a good one for relaxing. Bob, Chub and I still had moose tags to fill, but they could wait. The guides brought the meat in while the snow fell, and the thick fog made hunting near impossible. We rested our feet and watched the steam curl off the coffee. Every time we looked out the window, we were glad we had a roof over our heads.

In the morning, the clouds pulled back and we were ready to go. Omar and I set off right away, following a good, fresh track. Bob and Doug started upstream to the head of a large valley where they spooked a wolverine. Chub and his guide were headed for the tall timber. I returned to camp empty–handed, but Chub made a 250 yard shot on a 50–inch bull moose in the late afternoon.

Bob's guide, Doug had an interesting story to tell. They had been riding along the trail that led across a large flat rock. Stopping at the edge of the rock, Doug dismounted and told Bob to get down off his horse. He said he would never ride across a rock again.

Two years earlier he had guided a hunter from Pennsylvania. The man arrived in base camp overweight and out of shape. They rode ten miles to spike camp then ten miles more to the hunt area the next day. While crossing the rock, Doug's horse fell, pinning Doug's leg and breaking it in several places.

With his leg broken that way, there was no way he could survive the ten–mile ride out. He could feel himself going into shock and he couldn't move. The hunter from Pennsylvania looked down at his guide and his face turned white. He was scared to death, realizing that if his guide died out here, so would he. He leaned down to talk to Doug and Doug grabbed him by the front of his shirt and told him he had to get him covered with a blanket, gather wood, and get a fire started. The guide coached his hunter through building a fire. When there was enough wood stacked next to him and a good fire burning, Doug told the hunter he had to go for help.

The hunter had never been in the area before. The altitude and the cold was getting to him. Now he had to find his way ten miles back to spike camp. Grizzly bears or wolves might get him if he lost his way. And if he got lost, it was a cinch that Doug would die. "I don't know my way back," the client protested. "How will I ever find that little camp without you?"

"Look, dammit," Doug told him. "If you don't try, we're both going to die out here. All you have to do is follow the drainage down, back the way we came. It'll take you right back to camp, but it will take you some time to do it. You have to do this."

Fortunately, it was early in the day and the hunter was able to find the camp in the daylight. The camp cook mounted up and rode back to base camp for help.

Doug spent the whole night on that flat rock without so much as an aspirin, dozing and feeding the fire, gritting his teeth against the pain. In the morning, medics in a helicopter flew up the drainage, located Doug, and took him out to a hospital. With guides as tough as these, we were in good hands.

In the morning, Bob and Doug headed out on Chub and Barry's backtrail, hoping to spot one of the other moose Chub and Barry had seen on their way out the night before. They found it and Bob made another good shot, putting down a big bull moose with a 210–grain Partition.

I hurt my knee on the last day of the hunt. No one thought it would be a good idea for me to make the 12–mile ride back to the main camp, least of all, me. Thankfully, Terry was able to land his Super Cub on the meadow, and I made it to main camp way ahead of everybody else. It was nice to sit in a soft chair and warm my feet by the fire.

Chub and I headed out in front in Big Blue. Bob and Bill followed in Bob's Suburban. The road was icy, but Chub just rolled the power on. The road was straight as a string and pretty soon Bob's headlights were just little specks in Chub's rearview mirror.

We hit a patch of ice south of Wonowon, British Columbia. The truck swung sideways, seemingly in slow motion. Chub corrected, came out of the slide, then drifted the other way. I said to Chub, "We could end up in the ditch pretty soon." The truck drifted back the other direction and before we knew it we were upside down. 16 quarters of moose and elk, a stack of frozen backstraps, and five sets of elk and moose antlers weighed the old truck down and gave us the momentum that put us in the ditch. A wrecker arrived to pull us out, but all that meat and all those trophies were too much for one tow truck.

When Bob and Bill finally caught up to us, they chained up to the wrecker. Bob put the Suburban in low range and between the Suburban and the wrecker, they pulled Big battered Blue out of the ditch. We spent the night back in Wonowon.

"On the last day, sunlight sparkled like diamonds on the crusted snow and we had four good elk and three moose to show for our efforts." Front row, from left: Bill Board, Chub Eastman, John Nosler, Bob Nosler.

Bob and I finally pulled into Bend on the evening of October 30. We were happy to be home!

Later that year, I had a heart attack and my doctor sent me to Portland where I had a bypass operation. My heart specialist told me later that I would need another bypass. He insisted I go and get another bypass and straighten it out. I did. I wanted to be around to see the company weather its next challenge.

CHAPTER 27

Return to Family Ownership

Joining with Leupold and Stevens had been one of the best decisions I ever made. Their marketing and professionalism helped us bring our products to more people than ever before. But the mid–1980s brought several changes to the Leupold management team. Bob, Joan, Ron, Louise, and I talked about it. We were afraid our company might fall under the control of someone who had a different vision for our future.

Bob, who with Leupold, was Executive Vice President and General Manager of Nosler Bullets, set in motion a plan to return majority ownership in Nosler to the Noslers. The company had grown to approximately 50 employees. Our bullets had

The *Good Bullet Dad* ad represented the changing of the guard at Nosler. Young John and Bob took these nice bucks on the same day.

Good Bullet, Dad!

Young John Nosler shares his first successful mule deer hunt with his father Bob, President, and grandfather John, Founder and Chairman, Nosler, Inc.

■ Big game hunting is serious business in the Nosler family. It's a three generation, father-son tradition that has resulted in plenty of good times, lots of game, and development of the finest hunting bullet ever made. Nosler Partition®. ■ Designed for superior penetration and bone-crushing stopping power, Nosler Partition bullets have earned a world-wide reputation for anchoring trophy animals in their tracks. ■ Nosler's unique dual-core Partition construction and fully tapered jacket offers the hunter the ideal combination of deadly accuracy, controlled expansion and weight retention in any caliber, on any game, and in any situation. ■ Available at your dealer in popular hunting calibers and weights from 6mm through .375.

Nosler Partition
Bullets for Sportsmen®

For a free color catalog, call or write:
Nosler, Inc.
Box 671, Bend,
Oregon 97709
1 (800) 285-3701

1988 marked the return of full family ownership of Nosler, Inc.

From left: Fred Huntington (RCBS), John Nosler and Bob Stevens (Leupold and Stevens).

become the standard in the industry, and everyone who hunted big game knew our name. But we still had a lot of work to do.

In 1988, Leupold and Stevens were at a point where they wanted to invest more money in their other subsidiaries. The time was right. We made an offer to buy back their interest in our company. In December, ownership was returned to the family.

Chub Eastman, who had been a sales manager for Leupold, had become sales manager for Nosler along the way. When we bought Leupold out, Chub came with us and made the move to Bend. We were more than happy to have him.

I became Chairman of the Board and Bob became the President of Nosler, Inc. Both Joan and Ron took management/ownership roles with the company. We felt empowered and free. Louise and I couldn't have been happier.

John Nosler breaking ground at the new plant. Back row, from left: John Simonis, Greg Hawley, Chub Eastman, Bill Lewis, Ron Nosler, Alan Ashforth, Ed Neff and Bill Smith. Bob Nosler stands in the right foreground.

I set to work with a renewed vigor. I planned new products and worked on tooling up new machines. I engineered on yellow legal pads and took the drawings to the shop floor. Sometimes I was making changes to the drawings while the lead was still hot. Everybody in the shop contributed, because we all believed that a process could always be improved.

I loved the machinery. The sound of the presses running smoothly was like music to my ears. I worked in the shop and in the office. Our company was growing again and we were shipping more and more bullets overseas and to every part of the country.

But there was a shadow on the horizon. Within two years of the family taking over again, Louise – my most faithful business partner, my accountant and confidant, the one who answered the telephone, operated a bullet press, and helped me run the company – grew ill and passed away in 1991. How I missed her when she was gone.

John and Louise Nosler

CHAPTER 28

A Suit, a Clean White Shirt
and a New Bride

I turned over the management of the company to Bob after Louise passed away. He was ready for the responsibility and I could see it was his time.

I spent some time in southern California, renewing relationships with cousins, nieces and nephews, and old friends, but I was lonely.

One Sunday morning in June, I put on a suit, a clean white shirt, and went to the eight o'clock service at the Trinity Episcopal Church.

Vivian was on the altar guild and responsible for bringing flowers to the service every week. We knew each other because she had brought flowers for Louise when she was sick.

People who get up that early on a Sunday morning feel a kinship for each other. Those of us who go to the eight o'clock service all go out to breakfast afterward. Someone passes the word around that we'll meet at such and such a place and everyone shows up.

Vivian mentioned to me that everyone was welcome and I thanked her but suggested that she go to breakfast with me instead.

After breakfast, she drove home and I looked up a florist in the phone book. The next morning, a flower truck delivered a dozen long-stemmed roses to her door with my name written on the card. I called her a half-hour later and we had dinner together that night. Other dinners followed. I had already made up my mind. I wanted to marry her, but she kept calling me Mr. Nosler and suggested that we think about it again after Christmas. Christmas seemed a long way away.

Vivian had been alone for over three years. She was 70 and I was 79 and I was ready to get married again. She talked it over with her children and we discussed it over dinner many nights. We found that we thought the same way about a lot of things and had much in common.

On August 24th, 1992 we were married. 36 people showed up to celebrate with us. A minister, an organist and a florist came to do the service the way we wanted it. Vivian's sister and her husband supplied the orchid bouquets and boutineers. We followed the ceremony with a private dinner afterward.

Vivian was surprised that she would marry after such a short courtship. But she took a chance on me and I'm sure glad she did. She is a wonderful helpmate and I love her very much.

John and Vivian
Nosler

CHAPTER 29

Bullets, Ballistics, and Big Game

Choosing a Varmint Rifle

Today, varmint hunters have a wide range of centerfire rifles to choose from. From the 22 Hornet to the new super short magnums in 22 and 243 caliber. The 222 Remington has set accuracy records that will stand up with any of the modern cartridges. The 223 Remington is another good one. It is the choice of many varmint hunters and is the cartridge the US has used in the Armed Forces since the 1960's.

Once a year, several of us at Nosler Inc. head to Wyoming to thin down the prairie dog populations. We all take at least two rifles. I take a 223 and my old standby 22–250. When shooting at a good population of prairie dogs, two rifles are needed. One to shoot while the other one cools.

The 40–grain Ballistic Tip has become very popular for this work. The 223 is pushing that little pill at up to 3800 feet per second. With 28 grains of Benchmark powder, it goes up to 3860 feet per second. The 22–250 is way up to 4100 fps in some loads. When that 40–grain hits a prairie dog, there's just a little puff of hair left.

We are all waiting to see how the new 223 Winchester Super Short Magnum will do. The 22 BR Remington is close to the 22–250 for speed and the groups are very tight. Another favorite of mine is the 225 Winchester. It is fading in popularity as the 223 and 22–250 gain favor, but it has a great deal to offer. It has good velocity and is easy to load for accuracy. I used it a great deal for many years. I shot a good buck mule deer with it, loaded with the old Zipedo bullets we used to make.

Choosing a Big Game Rifle

The caliber of rifle you choose should fit you as well as the game you will use it on. It is much better to hit the game animal in the right place, with a rifle you can shoot well, than to hit it poorly with a large caliber rifle.

Many people are inclined to think bigger is better. Big sometimes is better as far as guns are concerned, but the shooter may never adapt to the recoil of the larger guns. His or her subconscious whispers, "this is going to hurt," the instant the brain tells the finger to squeeze the trigger.

Once a friend came to me and wanted me to look at his 300 Weatherby Magnum. He said the gun didn't shoot well anymore and he thought it needed a new barrel. I had a bench rest handy so I had him sit down in a comfortable position ready to shoot.

Still experimenting, John developed this fore–end stabilizer to help accurize his favorite 22–250 varmint rifle.

A few of John's rifles and the shooting medals he won in competitions. His early training with rifles prepared him for a lifetime of hunting adventure and bullet design.

I acted as if I loaded his rifle for him. But I didn't actually load it. Instead, I closed the bolt on an empty chamber. I handed him the rifle and told him to shoot when he was ready.

He yanked the trigger, jerking the barrel down as his subconscious told him the gun was going to hurt him. It was obvious what was wrong with his rifle. The problem was in his mind. For him, a rifle that kicked less and was fun to shoot would make him a much better shot on game.

If you have a heavy–kicking rifle and wish to continue hunting with it, shoot it as much as possible in practice to get used to the recoil. If the recoil is still a problem after a lot of practice, consider buying a different rifle. I used the pre–64 Model 70 in 300 H&H Magnum with 180–grain bullets for many years. I shot over 30 moose with that rifle, not to mention many deer, mountain goats, and more, but I know I still shoot tighter groups when I use the 270, 280, or 30–06.

Guns that are good on big game from pronghorns up to and including moose are the 257 Roberts, 260 Remington, 264, 270, 280, 308, and 30–06. The important thing is shot placement. The 243 loaded with a Partition bullet is a pleasant shooting rifle for deer–size game. I have used the 270 for elk several times with no problems, and I cannot remember shooting an elk with more than one shot.

I used the 300 Winchester Magnum a great deal and am convinced that the big 30 calibers will take a moose faster than the 7mm Magnum, but the 7mm Magnum is much easier to shoot. A well–placed shot with a smaller bullet will do a better job than a marginal hit with a 30 caliber. I think the worst thing a new shooter can do is to pick a gun that is too big for him or her to shoot well.

The 338 is a fine caliber when you have to use a bigger gun. Once we went to Alaska and I took my 338 as well as a 270 for sheep. I had been experimenting with muzzle breaks and I put one on the 338. It worked fine and made the gun nice to shoot as long as you wore earplugs. Your companions would also have to remember to keep out of the muzzle blast and stick their fingers in their ears.

We were taking a break from the hunt to do a little fishing, when our guide rode up on his horse and told me a nice grizzly was close by. We quit fishing and got on our horses, attempting to get far enough ahead of the bear so we could set up an ambush. But my 338 was back at camp. I had the 270 with me instead. I got up to

The Wall of Fame inside the bullet plant.

where we thought the grizzly would come out of the brush. I was somewhat worried because I wasn't sure that the 270 would stop a grizzly at ten feet.

There was a band of sheep close by and I kept an eye on them to see if they had caught the scent of the bear. After working the area, I was relieved to see the grizzly running away up the ridge, too far to shoot. I kept trying to get a grizzly but the ones we saw up close were too small, and the big ones were too far away.

If I had the time, I liked to shoot from the sitting position. Hunting on a hill, watching a canyon below, or the other hillside, you can drop down into a sitting position, rest your elbows on your knees and get rock–solid before you shoot.

Rifle Bullets

Today, after 56 years of production, the Partition bullet is used by more big game hunters than any other bullet. Its design is unique in that much of the front lead is released to fragment, causing tissue damage by the flying bits of lead. The folded

John R. Nosler and Bob with Bob's caribou taken on a hunt in September, 2001.

back, mushroomed bullet penetrates enough to most often exit the animal or be found just under the skin on the off side.

I have taken many large and small species of game. All have been quick kills as long as I did my part and hit the game in the vitals. The Partition bullet is excellent at long range, even on smaller big game, like antelope. It expands very fast for quick kills. I consider it to be two bullets in one. The forward half is for expansion and the rear portion is for penetration.

Our Ballistic Tip is made for hunting varmints and thin–skinned game such as antelope and deer. Because of its excellent ballistics, it is a good choice for use on game when long shots are a possibility.

It is a long bullet with a boattail and its weight is to the rear. It has a sharp plastic tip that resists deforming in magazines and retains its shape for utmost consistency, shot after shot.

"For big game, I think the worst thing a shooter can do is pick a gun that is too big for him or her to shoot well. A well–placed shot with a smaller bullet will do a better job than a marginal hit with a smaller caliber." – John Nosler.

Our Accubond is the new bullet that we have been working on for years. It employs an extruded jacket, which is thinner at the point and heavier in the mid–section. The jacket is gilding metal, an alloy noted for its ability to smoothly pass through the gun barrel. Like the Ballistic Tip, it sports a polycarbonate tip. The lead core is bonded to the gilding metal jacket by a secret process that we have developed over years of research and development.

On impact, it expands readily as the jacket is forced back by the impact of the tip. A portion of the lead core is exposed by the opening jacket and released to cause tissue damage and bleeding for quicker kills. At expansion, the bullet retains 70% to 80% of its weight, never going beyond two times its original diameter.

Beware of using bullets that expand in a large ball. Even if they don't lose any weight, they will seldom penetrate well.

A wide expansion is seldom good for deep penetration. Like our Partition bullet, the Accubond controls expansion to its optimum diameter and ensures deep penetration. Like the Ballistic Tip, the Accubond has a very good ballistic coefficient, which translates to a minimum loss of velocity at long range. The bonded core seems to work to tighten the group size for match–grade accuracy in a premium hunting bullet.

Making Long Shots

It is not a good idea to shoot at animals that are too far for a good, quick kill. But if you shoot a lot in practice, you can make a long shot now and then. I have done so much shooting in competition and in testing bullets that my hands and eyes are well–trained for long shots.

One time, two good friends and I were sitting down a ways in the Kiger canyon of Oregon's Steens Mountains. We had just witnessed a cougar slinking down through the brush below us, but no one took a shot because we were hoping to get a crack at a nice buck.

I began glassing the rims and spotted a large mule deer buck standing in the snow high up on a ledge a long ways away. I tried to point him out to my buddies, but it wasn't easy because he was so far away. He was standing in the bright snow in good light and was barely visible without field glasses.

"If I am in grizzly country I take with me a few cartridges loaded with the 150–grain Nosler bullet at around 2,950... There are other combinations just as good for sheep, no doubt, but I can't think of a better one." – Jack O'Connor on sheep hunting in *The Art of Hunting Big Game*

I must have wanted to show off, because I told my friends I was going to shoot him. I had my old tried–and–true 300 H&H pre–64 Model 70 with an eight–power scope. I held high, elevating the crosshair about six or seven deer above his back and squeezed the trigger. My friends were watching the deer through their field glasses and told me he dived off and down into the brush below.

A large area in the snow looked red. Anyway, I decided to go see if I did hit him. From the red–looking snow I was sure I had. It was a long rough climb to where he was, but I finally made it and, sure enough, there was blood in the snow. I found him dead down in the brush. Believe it or not, he was hit in the heart. We finally estimated the distance to be 900 yards.

The off–hand position and the sitting position are the two most useful positions for the hunter. Spend time shooting both ways in practice. I think I shot more game from the sitting position than any other way.

For precision shooting, the trigger pull is very important. You will shoot better if your trigger is smooth and crisp. For a hunting rifle, a three–pound pull is fine. It is best to have a gunsmith do the adjustment for you.

Prior to the hunt, I always check to see if my rifle is still zeroed. I've had things go wrong at the last minute – a scope spring can break, rifle primers might be bad, a scope mount might be loose – it's better to fix it on the range than to miss a shot and have to fix the problem in the field.

After the final sighting–in, I always clean the barrel and then try to fire one more shot. Think about it, when your rifle is zeroed, it is zeroed with a barrel that has been fired, not a barrel that has been cleaned after every shot. To be consistent, take the gun hunting after a round has been fired through a clean barrel.

Elk Hunting Tips

My grandparents were among the pioneers who settled the Oregon country. My dad was born on the trail and raised in the area near Coquille on the southern Oregon coast. They lived on elk in those early years. When I moved back to Oregon and I told my dad that I was going elk hunting for the first time, he said, "That's no sport. You might as well just shoot a cow in the field." In his day the elk ivory was valuable and used in jewelry and on watch fobs. My dad and a few others would get a wagon and a team of horses and get back up in the timber where they knew they could find elk. Then they'd start shooting. They took the elk teeth to sell and they took the best meat and they'd head for home. Times have changed.

I loved elk hunting right from the start. It was never as easy for me as it sounded like it was for my dad, but I learned a few things about hunting elk. I always found the biggest bulls in the highest country. Before and after the rut you could hear them bugling. Their calling helped me to locate them. As the rut progressed, the bulls tended to move lower, but I always had my best success when I hunted high, even when there was snow on the ground.

I liked to hunt saddles in the foothills. I walked the ridge tops slowly, looking for elk tracks. When I would come to a saddle, with great care I'd search it to see if I could find a trail that elk were using. If it looked like a crossing that elk used to move from one ridge to another, I knew I had a good chance to catch them there. If there were other hunters nearby, I knew my odds were even better if I stayed in one place and waited.

I learned to bugle to locate elk. I used my voice then, and would bugle or grunt or bark like an elk to call them in. Sometimes it worked and sometimes it didn't, but it was always worth a try. To call elk you have to have the wind in your favor. I liked to set up in cover with the wind in my face. I'd call, then listen and watch.

Another tactic we used sometimes was to drive the herd. If I was hunting with a group of people and I knew a ridge where we could find elk, I would position standers in the bottom of a draw and then work drivers down to them. The standers often had an opportunity and sometimes the drivers did too.

I hunted elk in thick timber on occasion. Elk often hide in thick pole patches or brushy country. Try still-hunting, moving slow through the trees along established elk trails, looking beneath the branches. Look for horizontal lines against the vertical trees, and look for dark legs. When you know you're close to elk, slow down and keep the wind in your face. Still-hunting in the brush can be a very effective way to get close to the animals.

Recent Hunts

I've had a number of great hunting partners over the years. In recent years, I've enjoyed hunting with Matt Smith. He is the son of my longtime friend, Bill Smith, who has been such a great help to us for so long.

When the leaves change color, when the smell of woodsmoke fills the air in October, when my breath turns to fog in the morning, I get that old urge to carry a rifle again. In 2002, it wasn't too hard for Matt to talk me into going deer hunting.

Matt picked me up on Wednesday afternoon. We loaded our gear, said goodbye to Vivian, and headed for the ranch. Instead of my favorite 7mm Magnum Remington Model 700, I carried my old Winchester Model 70 in 280 Remington.

The guys in the Ballistics Lab had loaded some Ballistic Tips and gave them to me for this trip.

We had about 45 minutes of light left when we pulled through the ranch's main gate. Matt had been watching a buck that had been using a nearby water hole. We set up near the water hole, but the big guy didn't come in. Instead, a 24–inch forked horn buck did. I wanted to take it, but Matt thought I might be able to get a bigger buck later in the hunt.

Finally, the sun went down and the buck wandered off. We spent the night in the cabin, eating last year's elk with onions and potatoes. I think Matt wondered how I was able to pack so much food away, but I was slipping some of it to little Amos, the dog. By the time we were ready for bed, Amos had decided I was his new best friend. When I headed for my bunk, the little dog sniffed out my bedroll and climbed right in, headed straight for the bottom of the bag. Well, there wasn't room enough for both of us, so Amos had to find another place to sleep.

It was cold and clear in the morning, with a stiff wind out of the North. Matt was excited about the prospects because a North wind made it easy to hunt one of his favorite spots, a nearby canyon.

We spotted quite a few elk right off the bat, glassed some smaller bucks and a few does. No one had hunted that canyon the whole year and it usually serves as a retreat for several good bucks, but for some reason we weren't seeing them this morning.

Matt was being careful to only look in places he thought we could both get to, but he couldn't resist taking a look up a nearby butte. When he did, he spotted a dandy buck, easing in and out of the bitterbrush, headed to the top of a large draw. His body was shaded and his antlers were in the sunlight. Matt was watching through his binoculars. I asked Matt how big he was and he held out his hands to show me. I could hardly believe it.

We tried to get closer so we might be in position when the buck reappeared, but he hadn't gotten that big by making stupid mistakes. He hid himself in a little fold in the landscape and then reappeared, walking casually toward the skyline. With his rangefinder, Matt marked him at 501 yards away. The big buck stopped to look back at us over his shoulder. I could tell Matt was kicking himself for not seeing the buck sooner. The buck had been bedded in the shadows among the tall bitterbrush and was certainly watching us the entire time.

Finally, the buck strolled over the crest of the hill and vanished out of sight into the head of a big draw. I said, "that sure was a nice buck, wasn't it Matt?" Matt thought about it a little bit and agreed that it was. "Sure seems a shame to let a buck like that just walk off. You better go see if you can get him."

I could tell Matt wanted to, but he didn't want to leave me to get a buck because this was supposed to be my hunt. I insisted. We had plenty of time. Besides, Matt might be able to go up the hill and push that deer down to me.

I stayed at the bottom of the draw while Matt cut around to the top to see if he could jump the buck and get it started down the hill toward me. Before he took off I told him, "Go ahead and shoot if you get the chance."

Matt headed out and around the top of the draw to keep the wind in his favor. He moved fast. I didn't think he had a lot of confidence that the plan would work, but he made a good try at it.

John with his buck taken on an Oregon mule deer hunt in 2002.

At the top of the draw, he found a small knoll that separated our draw from another that headed into the next drainage. So Matt moved around the knob to try and get a look at the buck through his binoculars.

He eased back around the knob to glass the draw I was watching. I waited while Matt peeked and poked around for quite a while. Being careful, he stayed in the shade, but staying in the shade kept him from seeing into one small fold of country. Finally, when Matt was beginning to walk into the draw, four panicked does erupted from over the ridge, coming from the neighbor's property. They almost ran Matt over and went right through the middle of the fold he couldn't see. As soon as they did, the big buck came out the other side, running low to the ground.

I heard Matt's first shot, quickly followed by a second. I could tell from the sound that both bullets had struck their mark. I knew he had bagged the big buck. Matt came down the draw with an "aw shucks" grin on his face.

Using a remote control camera, he was able to get us both in the picture and I was pretty proud to be there with him.

The rest of the morning we spent covering country and glassing hard with binoculars and my spotting scope. Again, we saw elk, antelope and mule deer, but no good bucks. We took a siesta during the warmest part of the day and headed out again for another try when the shadows started to grow. I was a bit worried about leaving Vivian another night so we found a place on top of a hill where we could get cell phone service. She said she was fine and that I should stay out one more night so I could get a buck. With that decided, we headed back to the water hole where we started the night before.

The forked horn buck was back, but he had three others with him and they were all bigger than he was. Unfortunately, the wind was wrong and the bucks knew we were there before they came too close, peering at us from over the top of a ridge. They trotted off around the hilltop and out of sight.

Skirting the hill, we got the wind in our favor and were able to approach the side of the hill by staying behind a low ridge at the base of the hill. The bucks were now in range but at the far end of what I wanted to shoot. The only problem was that the bucks had mingled with about 40 does. I was looking through my 8x scope but there were so many deer I couldn't tell which were bucks and which were does. Matt, using his 20x spotting scope picked one out and proceeded to try to describe his position to me.

The deer were headed up the hill and were going out of range. Then the buck Matt was describing to me stopped to take a bite of bitterbrush that was hanging over a ledge above him. Now the deer was by itself and I settled the stock into my shoulder. Matt wanted to get a little closer, but I didn't figure we needed to. I'd have to hold a little high to hit it at this range, but I had a pretty good rest, shooting at a buck standing broadside. I squeezed the trigger. Matt had a rangefinder with him and he told me how far it was. It was a long way out there.

Matt shot three rolls of film while I sat there next to my buck. I couldn't have been happier. 🌾

CHAPTER 30

Making the AccuBond

A few years ago we began to experiment with bonding a lead core inside our traditional copper–alloy jacket. We wanted to develop the next generation of high–performance bullets. We were able to bond the lead through a proprietary process to the jacket, eliminating voids in the bullet core. The result is a bullet that flies true, penetrates deep and retains about 65% of its weight. The copper–alloy material we use in the jacket does not copper–foul the rifle barrels like our competitors' bullets do.

After seven years in research and development we introduced the AccuBond in 2003, initially offering it for the 270, 7mm, 30, 338 and 375s.

With the introduction of any new Nosler bullet, we test and test and test. That means hours and hours in the Ballistics Lab. We shoot targets to test for ultimate accuracy.

To test for expansion, we still use racks of soggy newspapers occasionally, but it's not quite as handy as glue. Animal glue composition has the consistency of jelly and it kind of quivers a little. You heat it up and pour it in the mold. It does an excellent job but I still like using the newspaper tests occasionally.

After lab testing, we take the new bullets afield. The first generation of AccuBonds went to Wyoming with Bob, John R., Paul Coil (our CFO), Mike Lake (our plant manager), Paul Fortino (our attorney), Chuck Pritchard (our sales manager), and Chub. John shot the first animal at 50 yards with his handloaded 270.

Bob and John R, took Paul Coil and Mike Lake to the Nail Ranch in Texas where they shot feral hogs, and examined the wound channels to determine if the new bullet was performing as we hoped it would. The AccuBond produced clean, one–shot kills every time. The guides said they had never seen such clean kills on game.

Next, Bob, John R. and Layne Simpson hunted nilgai in Texas. The nilgai is an East Indian antelope that is bigger than an elk and one of the toughest animals on this continent to kill. They bagged three nilgai with three shots.

The AccuBond will give a weight retention of 75% when using standard velocity cartridges. When using the big magnums, expect a weight retention of about 65%.

I think you have to have a bullet soft enough that if you need to take a shot at 400 yards, you can hit your target and drop the animal right there. To do the job you need a bullet that won't go right on through, but expand. That's the part that I'm very particular about – that you still have expansion. It used to be that before, and during the war, I used a 30–06 a lot and I always said you could hit a deer with the '06 a long way away but you can't kill it. Back then, so many deer got away from

Nosler ballistics personnel load and fire hundreds of rounds per day in the course of testing samples from each production run.

Each Nosler bullet is inspected individually, assuring the utmost care in quality control.

Each punch press in the Nosler plant is custom–built in the company's tool and die shop.

Bullets from every run are tested to assure conformity to the company's strict production standards.

Samples from every production run are taken to the Ballistics Lab for testing. Because the ultimate test is in the field.

The ultimate test of any bullet is in the field. Here, Matt Smith (left), John and J.R. display the fruits of a high desert mule deer hunt.

guys that could hit. Our Partition bullet changed that and the AccuBond is the next step forward.

Since the 1950s, our bullets have been the standard of the shooting industry, the benchmark by which all other bullets are measured. The Nosler AccuBond, I believe, will be the benchmark for a whole new generation of premium bullets.

CHAPTER 31

On Business

The first fifteen years we were in business, Louise, Ron, and I had to do almost everything ourselves. No one could do the design work for me. I had to do it. That and the advertising, letter writing, calling distributors and dealers, trying to get them to stock the Partitions. I did all the buying of the materials, steel for the dies, copper, lead, lubricant, and everything else. At night, I read machine shop and engineering manuals in order to turn myself into an engineer.

As the business grew and we found people to work for us, I found it was a tremendous boon for employee morale to get our people involved in the shooting sports with us. We went target shooting, bird hunting, and big game hunting together when it was practical. It helped us get to know each other away from the plant and forge lasting relationships.

Every year a few of us went to Montana or Wyoming to hunt varmints. We took our management team to hunt deer and antelope on the Mankin Ranch in Gillette, Wyoming. We went several times and took quite a large crew with us. The first time we went we held a shoot–off the first morning. Everyone knew it was coming. You had one shot. The wind was blowing hard and it was raining. We set the target out at 200 yards. Everyone in our crew could shoot, but the conditions were bad. Everybody took their turn. Most shots were within two or three inches of the bull. Ed Neff placed his bullet right up against the bull and thought he was going to win the match. When my turn came up, I pulled the rifle tight into my shoulder and drilled the bull.

The outfitter wouldn't let you go hunting until you proved to him that you could shoot. You had to hit the gong, a metal disk, about the size of a basketball, down in the canyon behind the house. You had to shoot from the top of the canyon and make that sucker ring with a 200–yard shot. They wouldn't let you even get in the truck until you hit it.

We all hunted and took both deer and antelope. The ranch owner was born and raised there and knew everybody in the area. He'd go to any ranch we'd ask him to take us to. Antelope were no problem to find. But the deer seemed to prefer one type of habitat.

The ranchers pointed us to these huge washes, maybe a mile wide, that were graded off for farming. Alfalfa was planted in the washes. The washes were down 20–50 feet below the common elevation. All you would have to do is find a wash and there was always a herd of deer in it. We would hunt other places but nothing was as productive as those areas.

I liked to think that every employee was a part of our team. I promised them 40 hours pay and, in return, they promised me 40 hours of work. We all worked hard

John R. Nosler with a trophy caribou taken in the Northwest Territories in 2001.

North America's pronghorn antelope, once on the verge of extinction, is now well–represented in our western states. It is just one example of many where hunters' dollars have made the difference for wildlife. "We must take our children and grandchildren to hunter education classes, then take them hunting. We must support scientific game management and turn back attempts at managing wildlife through the ballot box." – John Nosler

J.R. (left) and Bob celebrate the end of a successful caribou hunt in the Far North.

to keep our ends of the bargain. Sometimes when a piece of equipment was broken and production was down, instead of sending them home, Louise and I would send a few employees up to the house to do yardwork or painting, so that the employees would get full paychecks.

I would never ask an employee to do something I wasn't willing to do myself. If the floor needed sweeping and the shop maintenance crew was working on something else, I would do it for them.

The most important thing we did was to keep the employees interested in the shooting sports. I didn't require that they were NRA members, but I sure hoped they were. I insisted that every employee know our products and how they should be used. Every employee is a representative of the company away from work. They

Nosler's management team stays in touch with every aspect of bullet production and quality control. Here John (left) and Bob inspect bullets coming off one run of Ballistic Tips.

"To succeed in business, you have to find something you can do well. That's the biggest chore. Then decide to do it and don't let anything stop you. Keep fighting and pushing."
– John Nosler

should, I believed, be able to speak with knowledge and confidence about any of our products.

To succeed in business you have to find something you can do well. That's the biggest chore. Then decide to do it and don't let anything stop you. Keep fighting and pushing.

CHAPTER 32

Constitution and Community— Looking to the Future

I still go into my office at the plant almost every day. I love to see my sons and grandchildren working in the business. One of my greatest pleasures is having lunch with an old friend and swapping stories. I love to read the mail and look at pictures of game that hunters all over the world have taken with our bullets. Someday I may retire, but I'm only 90 and I have a lot of good years ahead.

I have enjoyed working on my dream of better bullets and bringing them to the world. The marketplace today is much different than it was when we started out. I'm thankful that I live in this great country where I have had the opportunity to reach for my goals. We were created to live free and pursue our dreams, and I am proud to be an American. The hunt, and hunting have kept me fit, strong, and healthy.

There is a vocal minority that seeks to destroy our way of life. The best way, the only way to fight them is to join with like–minded individuals to confront them and fight for our rights at every turn. We must educate the public about our Constitution and our Bill of Rights. We must take our children and grandchildren to hunter education classes, then take them hunting. We must support scientific game management and turn back attempts at managing wildlife through the ballot box.

Take a non–hunting friend target shooting, then take them afield. Join or start hunter organizations and get representation at local and state levels. Join the NRA and other shooting sports groups and stand firm against those who would take our rights away.

My son Ron, after spending many years at the plant, has retired from the bullet business and owns a painting company, which keeps him busy. His work, since those first days in Ashland, went a long way toward making our company what it is today.

My son Bob is active in our community and with the National Rifle Association. He is well known and well liked in the industry, more so than I now. Just the other day I was in the den fooling around and I ran across his little leather pouch that would hold one packet of cartridges on his belt. Inside was a little over half a box of 250–3000 Savage ammunition loaded with old Nosler Partitions from the 1950s. I looked at those bullets and I smiled, knowing the company is in capable hands, still producing those bullets, today with a lot more efficiency than in those early days.

My grandson John R was a good high school and college football player. He still helps to coach track and football with his old high school coaches, but is working

John R. Nosler with a Texas Aoudad that fell to an AccuBond bullet.

Jeff and Jill (Nosler) Bailey with Jill's first trophy hog on a 2003 hunt on the Nail Ranch in Texas.

John and Matt Smith with Matt's Oregon mule deer from their 2002 hunt.

in the plant with us now, playing for our team. He has already made some good contributions to Nosler Inc.

JR took his first antelope in Wyoming when he was 14. He was raised among hunters and well–educated about guns and he knows how to use them better than a lot of old timers. After that Wyoming hunt he went with us on as many hunts as he could, school schedules permitting. In 2001, Bob and JR made a trip to the Far North to hunt for caribou. They came back with two very nice bulls.

JR is taking over the management of Nosler's advertising and marketing functions and he also manages our retail store at the plant. I am very proud of the man.

Today we make the best sporting bullets in the world. I'm guessing that if better bullets than these are ever made, they will be made right here at our plant in Bend, Oregon.

Big John and J.R. Nosler at the end of their October 2003 Oregon mule deer hunt. John used his favorite 280 Remington on this hunt.

222

To date, we have produced five Nosler Reloading Guides. The most recent was published in 2002. Not only are we dedicated to supplying shooters with top quality bullets, we are committed to providing the best information available for our customers.

I have a precious wife, Vivian. We have fun doing what we both like and that includes most anything as long as we're together. I have two sons of whom I am proud. Three grandchildren: Christie Darcy, Jill Bailey, and John R. Nosler. I can't get enough of my great–grandchildren: Jordan, Karli, Joel, Zackery, and Emalie.

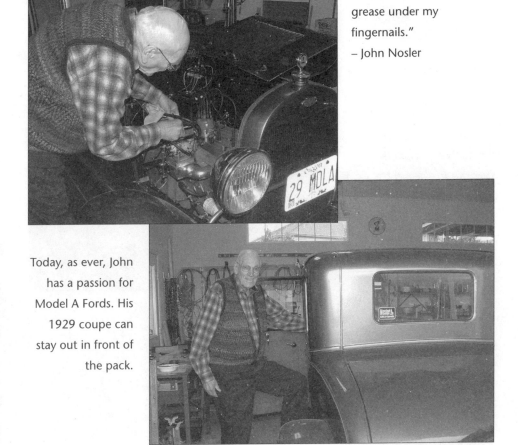

"There's still some grease under my fingernails."
– John Nosler

Today, as ever, John has a passion for Model A Fords. His 1929 coupe can stay out in front of the pack.

I still shoot now and then, though I have given almost all of my guns away. I confess, the Ballistic Tip and AccuBond are probably the most accurate bullets we make, but I still like to shoot a Partition when I have a big buck or bull in my sights.

I like to work on my old 1929 Ford Coupe, keeping her shined and running. I'm a member of the Model A club in central Oregon. We drive our old cars on trips around the country. I know a few tricks that keep my old Model A out in front of the pack. And I still have a little grease under these fingernails.

Editor's note:

The National Rifle Association and Nosler, Incorporated have established the John A. Nosler Endowment Fund to promote marksmanship and firearms training. Tax–deductible donations are welcome. Write to John A. Nosler Endowment Fund, NRA Foundation, 11250 Waples Mill Road, Fairfax, VA 22030.

CHAPTER 33

Back to the Territories—
60 Years Later By Gary Lewis

The creak of old leather. Blued metal and walnut stocks. Wool hunting coats. The clip–clop–clip–clop of the pack strings' hooves on the trail. An untamed river, winding its way to the ocean. And the bellow of a bull moose in the willows.

The hunters heard him across the river. He grunted a challenge – a lone bull, looking for a fight. His wide antlers slapped through the trees and the willows parted before him. The guide saw him first.

"Oh. Big bull," Ted Hayes said. The moose was across the river, his antlers just visible now above the willows. A moment later, he stepped into the open. He was in range, but as young John Nosler steadied for the shot, the bull turned and headed straight toward the hunters. He was grunting as he came on, splashing through the tailout of a pool, crossing the river now.

"Nobody move," Ted whispered.

As it was in 1946, so it was 60 years later in 2006 when John R. Nosler and Bob Nosler followed once again in the footsteps of the elder Nosler.

The boundary of the frontier is farther north than it used to be. There are still moose where John A. Nosler found them in 1946, but for the 60–year anniversary, Bob and J.R. Nosler wanted to go deep into the wilderness. They found it in the Yukon.

Bob and J.R. began to plan the Nosler 60th anniversary moose hunt in 2004, two years in advance. It took almost that long for Bob to locate the right rifle. He would carry an early Model 70 Winchester 300 H&H stoked with antique Nosler Partitions (as Bob says, "My dad made them and my mom packaged them, so I know they're old.") J.R. Nosler would carry a new Nosler Custom Model 48 325 WSM with an appetite for AccuBonds.

Bob waited with Layne Simpson, while airlines and Customs officials waited for Simpson's rifle to show up. The rest of the party, led by Lone Wolf Outfitters guide Wes Phillips, began the long ride to camp.

18 miles out from the trailhead, the horses began to get nervous. In fact, the trail looked like a virtual bear highway as it climbed out of the Fish Lake drainage. J.R. saw a grizzly top out on a little ridge. Its chocolate pelt shone in the sunlight and the silver–tipped hair rippled in the wind. Grabbing his rifle from the scabbard, J.R. bailed out of the saddle, made the stalk and shot the bear at the up–close–and–personal range of 55 yards.

The next day, the hunters rode up through Ozzy's Pass to a vantage point where they could glass several miles of tundra. But the wind blew hard from the North and it was difficult to keep the glass anchored.

This is game country, but it is bigger than most people can fathom. The Yukon is bigger than some European countries and most U.S. states. It is a mega–wilderness of mountains, little clumps of fir trees, pothole lakes and patches of willows, home

18 miles out from the trailhead, the horses began to get nervous. John R. (J.R.) Nosler bailed off the horse and grabbed his Model 48. The grizzly bear topped out on a little ridge and stood his ground.

to 50,000 moose, 150,000 caribou, 22,000 mountain sheep, 10,000 black bears, 10,000 wolves and 7,000 grizzlies.

When the wind forced the hunters to shift positions, they found shelter on the side of the hill and Phillips produced a tube of moose sausage and a block of cheese.

It wasn't long before someone spotted a lone bull moose bedded a mile away across the canyon, and then Jim Kinsey spotted another moose.

While they were watching the moose, Wes spotted a caribou and the hunters made a stalk, using the mountain as cover. When next they saw the bull, he was standing in a thicket of small trees—250 yards away. John dropped to one knee, found the sight picture and squeezed. He was a big bull with double shovels, back–scratchers and heavy main beams. As John Andre said, it's a matter of covering ground with your eyes, not covering ground on your feet.

That evening, they spotted a second big caribou and the stalk took the hunters a little closer than they'd expected. Cresting a small ridge, they surprised the big bull and a record–book mountain caribou at 30 yards. The herd broke away and started into the canyon. John Andre's second 200–grain AccuBond connected, and a third put the bull down for good.

Optics are the answer in big country. Guide Wes Phillips spotted this nice bull. After a long stalk, J.R. dropped to his knee and made the 250–yard shot.

The next morning, the sky was clear, blue and cold. Fall was in the air and the next phase of the hunt was beginning. It would start with an 18–mile ride off the mountain. It was time to find a moose.

Bob had finally made it to camp with Layne Simpson. Bob's guide would take him upstream in a jet boat in search of a big bull moose they'd seen the day before. A jet boat makes navigating the shallow rivers a lot easier. Sometimes the hunters had to stop to clean the rocks out of the pump. At the end of the day, they found a nice bull standing in the river. The bull, which was wide, between 50 and 55 inches from tip to tip, splashed across the river and climbed up on the opposite bank. He turned broadside and gave Bob one last chance. "We'll let him get a little bigger," Bob decided. The bull continued on in search of a cow as the hunters drifted downriver.

"The moose is our history," Bob said later. It was moose hunting on the frontier— In places like British Columbia and the Yukon and Alaska—that was the catalyst that started John Nosler down the road to build bullets which would forever alter the course of of big game hunting. In our changing world, there are some places, some things that don't change. And you can find them in the Far North—hunting the way it was 60 years ago.

On the 60th anniversary hunt, Bob and J.R. celebrate J.R.'s first grizzly.

Bob would spend the next five days hunting upstream on the Wolf River, while J.R. and John Andre would go downstream, by canoe, to a cabin 25 miles away. Three canoes, two guides, two hunters, and a cameraman to record the hunt. One of the guides was Ted Hayes, a two–time World Champion moose caller.

The leaves on the willows were golden. As the canoe paddles dipped and paused after each stroke, droplets of water ran down the paddle and bent the reflection of the untamed wilderness. Every turn in the river opened a new window into the forest and a chance to surprise a bull on the river bank.

This part of the river had not been hunted since 1994. Soon the hunters spotted a cow in the river, feeding in the weeds. Ted called a stop and tried to call in a bull, if one was nearby.

Beavers worked at building their lodges before winter and ducks preened along the bank. Hayes stopped and called at some of the likely spots and on the second day of the float, finally, an answer. But no bull materialized from the willows.

In the evening, Jeff McNaughton called in a bull. He had a cow with him and he didn't want to come out of the willows, but come he finally did, on the run. The cow popped out of the brush first and then the bull followed. And Andres' shots connected.

By morning, clouds had begun to form in the sky and there was new snow on the mountains. J.R. and Ted Hayes found a spot in the corner of the river where Ted's calls could reach into a series of draws.

Suddenly a calf moose showed up, just across the river and then just as quickly it was gone again. A moment later, a cow moose showed up, looking for the calf. She looked across the river and spotted J.R. and the cameraman. And then a young bull moose, fully in the grip of the rut, stepped out of the willows. Following the cow, his neck outstretched, his tongue scent–checked the wind. But J.R. was looking for a bigger bull.

That evening, the wolves moved in and the moose moved off. It was time to change the strategy. The hunters began to focus on drawing in moose that were on the move, headed down, out of the mountains.

As the sun moved toward the horizon, Ted Hayes changed his strategy. Instead of using cow calls, he'd challenge the bulls to a fight and see what would happen.

With little more than an hour of light left, a moose answered. J.R. sensed something was about to happen. Then the wind shifted, blowing their scent toward the sound of the oncoming bull. And away off in the distance came the whine of a jet boat motor. Whatever was going to happen was going to happen fast.

"Let's go," Ted said. They headed straight toward the sound of the approaching bull, moving faster than the breeze that was at the back of their necks.

"Oh. Big bull," Ted said. The moose was across the river, his antlers just visible now above the willows. A moment later, he stepped into the open. He was in range, but as J.R. steadied for the shot, the bull turned and headed straight toward the hunters. He was grunting as he came on, splashing through the tailout of a pool.

"Nobody move," Ted whispered. In less than a minute, the bull had crossed the river, grunting all the way. He stood on the gravel bar, quartering toward the hunters, then went broadside.

At the impact, John's first shot blew a spray of water from the bull's flanks as the AccuBond went right through the vitals. The second shot, for insurance, went in the same place and the bull stumbled out of the tall grass and died in the water.

Back at the main camp, Bob also completed his moose hunt. The old Partitions, built by Dad and packaged by Mom, worked just as well as they did in 1946.

More than 60 years have passed since the hunt that started it all. Many things have changed, but in the Far North, the hunt is as it has always been. It is easy to see what it was that drew John Nosler and other sportsmen of the 1940s and 1950s to hunt moose in the wilderness. It is that same call to adventure that draws us there today.

60 years after Big John designed and built his first Partitions, Nosler Inc. is known worldwide for the bullets produced in Bend, Oregon, USA.

Today's catalog features the Partition, the Partition–HG handgun hunting bullet, the E–Tip lead–free bullet, the Nosler Solid, the AccuBond, the Ballistic Tip, the CT Ballistic Silvertip, the Nosler Custom Competition bullet and the Sporting Handgun bullet.

This bull answered a challenge, looking for a fight. It pushed through the willows across the river, waded through the current, then trotted out onto the gravel bar. John hammered it with an AccuBond from the Model 48.

Bob Nosler celebrated the 60th Anniversary of Nosler bullets in the Northwest Territories with a 300 H&H and an antique Nosler Partition bullet.

The latest addition to the line is the E–Tip. Bob Nosler recognized the need for this bullet more than a decade ago and development and testing has been underway for years. "The new Nosler E–Tip is a lead–free bullet that doesn't compromise on accuracy, expansion, or penetration. We've put many, many hours into every step of the process leading up to its initial release. The field tests proved that all the time in development really paid off, we even surprised ourselves and we knew we had a superior product! The expansion is incredibly uniform while still retaining 95%+ of its weight. The only problem we experienced during the field test was recovering a sample. No matter what they hit, they punched right through."

30 caliber (.308) Nosler Ballistic Tip Hunting Bullets.

22 caliber (.224) Nosler Ballistic Tip Varmint Bullets.

The solid copper alloy Nosler E–Tip Bullet uses a polycarbonate tip to initiate expansion into the energy cavity, providing stopping power and uniform expansion with about 95% weight retention.

The Nosler Partition Bullet.

Handloading is a part of the Nosler heritage and John's quest for accuracy and performance is reflected in NoslerCustom a division of Nosler, Inc. Custom loading goes hand–in–hand with producing world–class projectiles. At Nosler, they've been handloading for personal hunts and for the day–to–day accuracy and ballistics testing process that has always been vital to the manufacturing and quality control of their premium bullet lines. 60 years of working up the right load for the right cartridge, using the right powder, the right primer and putting it all together with the right bullet, they've learned how to craft ammunition that is accurate and consistent.

NoslerCustom cartridge brass is built to the exacting standards of a company committed to accuracy and consistency. Each case comes with flash holes deburred and checked for proper alignment. Each case is hand–inspected and sorted by weight. Case mouths are chamfered and deburred and prepped—ready to reload.

NoslerCustom Ammunition is true premium ammo produced by expert handloaders. Cases are checked for correct length, necks are sized, chamfered and trued, flash holes are checked for alignment, powder charges are meticulously weighed and finished rounds are hand–inspected and hand–polished. Loaded rounds are packaged in hard plastic boxes with performance data printed on the

The Model 48 Sporter is a tribute to Big John and the year 1948 when he began selling his first Partitions.

label. Ammunition boxes can be personalized with the customer's name at no additional cost.

The Model 48 Sporter is a tribute to Big John and the year he began selling his new Partitions. This rifle is built for the hunter. With a Kevlar composite stock, the Sporter tips the scale between 6.25 pounds and 6.5 pounds. The stock's onyx–gray finish is complemented by a sniper–gray ceramic coating on the barrel and action. The company guarantees an accuracy of three–quarters of an inch at 100 yards.

NoslerCustom also produces a line of gun safes, designed and constructed to the highest industry standards. The safes can be individually serial numbered to match the serial number on the Custom rifle.

The Gold Standard of Accuracy

We have a shooting range east of our town. We call it COSSA, short for Central Oregon Shooting Sports Association. It has been our collective dream to put a thousand–yard range on the property. In 2007 the dream became a reality.

We christened it the John Nosler Thousand Yard Range.

To dedicate the facility, COSSA President Bill Fockler invited Big John, now in his mid–90s, to fire a few bullets downrange.

Limited to just 500 total units per series, the NoslerCustom Rifle offers an accuracy guarantee of one–half inch three–shot groups at 100 yards when loaded with NoslerCustom hunting loads and AccuBond bullets.

Bill Lewis painted a 4x8 sheet of plywood bright–white and overlaid a 40–inch black circle for the target. 1000 yards with a .30–06 is no easy shot. At that distance, a bullet will drop more than 35 feet, necessitating a hold–high of 400 inches or more. A five–mph wind could blow the bullet four feet off–course.

A few people said nice things about Big John and then he took the bench, pulling the butt of the .30–06 into his shoulder. He pushed a green–tipped Nosler into the chamber, locked it home and found the target in the Leupold scope.

It was 1:00 in the afternoon. We had a light crosswind. John held on the outside left of the 40–inch circle and the gun spoke. A few people clapped. John chambered

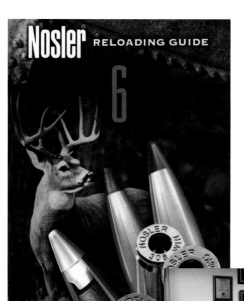

The Nosler Reloading Guide Number Six features 117 cartridges. Each cartridge is introduced with personal experience, advice and anecdotes from some of the world's best– known hunters, shooters and writers.

Jeff Bailey (left) and Mark Roberts in the Boardroom. Bailey is Director of Supply Management and Roberts is Vice President/Business Manager.

another round and looked back at Bill. Bill had his eye to the spotting scope. "Same hold, John."

John tucked into the rifle, held left–side of the black and squeezed. A thin wisp of dust was visible, over half a mile away.

John posed for pictures and shook hands with a few youngsters and then everyone left for home. Everyone except for Bill Lewis.

Bill cased the rifle, folded up the shooting bench and drove downrange to secure the target. He found two holes in the black at nine o'clock. Two holes nine inches

Continued on page 240.

John Nosler continued to hunt moose in the Far North into the 1980s, but one thing he always wanted to do was take his bullets to Africa. Of course, Nosler bullets had been going to Africa since the early 1950s, but it wasn't until the 21st Century that Noslers carried Nosler bullets to South Africa. For his first Cape Buffalo, Bob Nosler used a 416 Remington Magnum with 400–grain Partitions and a 400–grain Nosler Solid.

Chuck Pritchard, Nosler's Sales Manager, carried his 338 Winchester Magnum to South Africa and felled this big bull gemsbok with a 250–grain Partition.

Bob Nosler and J.R. celebrated the family's 60th year in the bullet business right back where it all started on a moose hunt in the Far North. Bob used an old Winchester Model 70, chambered in .300 H&H Magnum and bullets built by his dad and packaged by his mom. For his hunt, J.R. chose the .325 WSM and a Model 48 with an appetite for AccuBonds.

J.R. with a big black bear from British Columbia.

J.R. Nosler took his first Cape Buffalo on his second trip to Africa in 2007.

Nosler Plant Manager Mike
Lake with a Texas hog.

Jeff Bailey with the
mule deer buck
he tagged on a
Wyoming hunt.
Nosler bullets are
built by sportsmen
for sportsmen.

Big John and J.R. Nosler at the end of their October 2003 Oregon mule deer hunt. John
used his favorite 280 Remington on this trip.

apart, with about two inches difference in elevation. At a thousand yards that equates to less than one–minute–of–angle, the gold standard of accuracy.

John Nosler still loves to shoot and he looks forward to those October days on the desert. But most days, he can be found in his office at the plant in Bend, Oregon or turning wrenches on his Model A Ford. The young barefoot farm boy in overalls has become a legendary sportsman and innovator. Generations of hunters and target shooters use the bullets that bear the Nosler name.

His work in the field of projectile performance prompted the development of the premium bullet industry that employs thousands across the country and satisfies shooters around the globe. In everything John Nosler has done, he has driven to be his best. It shows in his company's products, his love of accuracy and his decision for precision. 🦅

Mark Roberts, Nosler CFO, hunted in South Africa with some of the first Nosler E–Tip bullets. He used a NoslerCustom 300 WSM rifle.

John Nosler, wearing a vintage Nosler cap, helped to dedicate a 1000–yard shooting range in central Oregon last spring, while Gary Lewis and Bill Lewis look on. Nosler used a 1903–A3 Springfield, fitted with a Leupold Mark IV 10–power. Photo courtesy Greg Gulbrandsen.

Acknowledgements

What started out as a way for me to provide high–quality bullets for my hunting partners has turned into quite a business. It was first a labor of love and then it became a way of life. The success of the company now called Nosler, Inc. is due in part to the friends I met and made along the way. It is due in part to the dedicated employees who were a part of the company in the early years and to the employees who make the company what it is today. I value each and every one of you.

Words could never express the depth of my appreciation for the people who have been a part of this dream of building better bullets. It would be impossible for me to remember each and every one here and it would be even more difficult to list them in any kind of order. But my life has been richer because you were a part of it.

Jack James, Tom Alley, Marion Mann, Bob Mace, Dr. Walt Weller, John Henderson, Edith Henderson, Fred Huntington, Buzzy Huntington, Louise Nosler, Ronald Nosler, Robert Nosler, Joan Nosler, John R. Nosler, Vivian Nosler, Jill Bailey, Jeff Bailey, Hal Swiggett, Rick Jamison, Edward Matunas, Clay Harvey, Layne Simpson, Francis Cheney, Dick Alley, Don Brace, Bob Van Vleet, Don O'Bleness, Con Fury, Clarence Purdy, Walt Remmy, Guy Lewis, Roy Banta, John Prehn, Ray Wade, Jack O'Connor, Elmer Keith, Warren Page, Joyce Hornady, Elgin Gates, Vernon Speer, Paul Leerson, Alan Ashforth, Gail Root, Gene Caron, Ed Neff, Mark McConnell, Charles Flack, Tracy Lantz, John Simonis, Eric Hansen, Chub Eastman, Bill Lewis, Terri Bergstrom, Connie Roach, Franky Swanzy, Eric Mandich, Matt Smith, Bill Smith, Pat Metke, Paul Coil, Mike Harris, Chuck Pritchard, Mike Lake, Trygve Bolken, Mike Napierkowski, Mickey Figueroa, Mark Roberts, Paul Fortino, Jack Durret, Bob Marchant and Gary Lewis.